Heaven Helps
Those Who Help Themselves

MARKEITH SAMS

Fulton Books, Inc.
Meadville, PA

Published by Fulton Books 2023

ISBN 979-8-88982-002-4 (paperback)
ISBN 979-8-88982-003-1 (digital)

Printed in the United States of America

INTRODUCTION

I have always been very adamant about speaking on African American issues in America. For as long as I can remember, I have been hell-bent on fixing what is wrong with B lack America. There are many issues that affect the African American community that are not being addressed adequately. For a long time now, many African American people have been under the impression or made to feel that they are helpless and need to depend on someone on the outside to help them rebuild their communities. Of course, this is not true. No one from the outside is coming to help rebuild a community in which they do not live. It is time for us as Black people or African Americans in this country to take responsibility for our own neighborhoods and our own schools and our own economics and our own future. It is time for us to stop wasting time complaining about injustices that have been done to us in the past. It is time for us to realize that our future is in our own hands.

We, as African Americans, have everything that we need to succeed. We have access to free education, food stamps, financial assistance, housing assistance, and whatever other kind of assistance you can think of to help us to rise out of poverty and into the middle class. Those who choose to take advantage of the resources around them find that it is not extremely hard to achieve more in life. It is now five decades past the Civil Rights Movement, yet African Americans have not made as much progress as we should have in America. Granted, a lot of African Americans have been able to rise out of poverty by attending college and becoming employed in career fields that have made it possible for them to live and raise their children as part of the middle class. The mere fact that many have been able to do so means that, in theory, everyone else with the same amount of effort and hard work and motivation should be able to do the same.

Today's inner-city neighborhoods are falling apart, literally falling in on themselves. Houses that are mostly vacant or dilapidated have taken over the neighborhoods. The only people who live in these run-down neighborhoods are those who cannot afford any better. I am sure if they had the means, they too would move out of these run-down areas that are crime-filled, drug-infested cesspools. However, they do not have the resources to get out, so they say. The truth is they do have the resources to get out. They have always had the resources to get out, but they have not taken advantage of those resources. There are countless social service agencies and community organizations throughout America located in every major locale and medium-sized city whose main objective is to help uplift those who live in poverty and help them to live a better life. I mean, there are literally people who go to work every day wanting to help make someone else's life better, but for each and every one of them who want to help, there are just as many, if not more, of those within the African American community who either abuse the help, misuse and defraud the help or act as though they are forever entitled to the help, and those who simply do not know about the help.

Our neighborhoods are not growing. We are neither renovating these older neighborhoods with old houses nor building new houses; therefore, eventually, these neighborhoods are going to become completely vacant or taken over by drug gangs and crack fiends. Crime in the inner city has driven the businesses away and the banks who loan money. Those who are interested in trying to reinvest in these neighborhoods cannot get loans to do so because of the crime rate in these neighborhoods. This is known as *r edlining*, something that many know little about.

Gentrification is one solution to solve the problem of the inner city and begin to rebuild these older run-down neighborhoods, but African Americans who live in these areas who are subject to being gentrified are opposed to the idea of their neighborhood being rebuilt by people who do not look like them. So who do they prefer? What do they suggest? Why are they opposed to the idea of having their neighbors receive the help that they need to become marketable and grow? Many say that it is because they are afraid that they will be pushed out of their neighborhoods and forced to relocate to other parts of town that remain affordable to them once the new construction and business developments raise the market value of their existing neighborhood. I do not believe that gentrification must necessarily displace the people who currently live in the neighborhoods who have the most need for revitalization. It is my belief that the people living in these neighborhoods should willingly work with those in government to work on plans for revitalizing their neighborhoods and bringing in new businesses and jobs to their community. But, I believe, to do this, they must realize that they have the power to make things happen. They must understand that they must take an active role in what happens to their neighborhoods. It is now time to act and for them to speak up for what they want to have happen in their neighborhoods for their children and their grandchildren to come. If they do not do it, then who will?

Although a great deal of Black people in America have made much progress, there are many who continue to live the same as they were before the Civil Rights Movement. African Americans continue to lag White Americans in education and housing and employment. The unemployment rate has consistently been twice the White unemployment rate (Federal Reserve Economic Data 2020). Why is this? Why are we continually on the bottom? Why are our academic achievement and employment rates much lower than that of Whites and Asian Americans? Is it because we do not value education, or is it because we simply cannot perform at the level they do?

It is my belief that African Americans are incredibly talented, naturally so, and can learn and outperform anyone whom we are put up against when we put forth our absolute best efforts. I feel that many African Americans do not perform at their optimum level because they feel that doing so is somehow acting White. Why do we feel that being educated and speaking proper English is acting White? Who decided that? Where did this notion come from? Is being ignorant and ghetto associated with being Black? Is that what we think of ourselves?

For us to thrive as a community and prosper, we must figure out the answers to these questions and understand why we do not force ourselves to live up to our full potential. It is up to us and only us to better our situations and rebuild our communities. Education is how we've achieved success; therefore, we must take it seriously and fight for our schools to properly educate our children and to ensure that they are college- and career-ready when they leave high school. All too often, African American students do not achieve on grade level but are passed on to the next grade, year after year. Doing so places them at a greater disadvantage when they enter college or the workforce.

The last thing African American students need is to be passed along from grade to grade without having learned what it is they need to know at each level. Education builds upon itself; when you have not learned what you were supposed to in the third grade, it will show in the fourth, fifth, and sixth grade and so on and so forth, all the way through high school. The education system is doing our children a great disservice by making it easy on them and allowing them to be passed along when they have not achieved on their grade level and proven that they are ready for the next grade. The No Child Left Behind Act put in place by President George W. Bush's administration has done more harm than good. It was intended to help close the achievement gap between African American and White students but, in fact, has made matters worse and failed to achieve the desired effect.

There are many disparities between the African Americans and White Americans, most of them obvious while others remain obscure. Education has always been considered by most African Americans to be the master key for unlocking the doors of inequality; however, education alone cannot free a slave. For nearly 403 years, African Americans have been the underclass in American society except for a minute upper-class and a slightly larger middle-class population. There are possible explanations for such an unequal education. Is it the result of underfunded schools or the more propagated theory that relies on discrimination and years of oppression by White America? Although these theories do hold significant weight in this ongoing argument, I feel that they fail to expose a more deeply rooted and persistent cause. Could Black culture be the culprit? Is African American culture the cause of the disparities that exist between the African American community and White America?

Within the African American community, there exists high crime rates that stem from high poverty rates that are the result of high unemployment rates and high school dropout rates. Even though these negative statistics are evident, inner-city African American communities carry on like nothing is wrong. I tend to feel like the majority of African Americans feel like there is nothing that can be done about all these. On the contrary, there is plenty that can be done to sort out this horrible mess that we currently find ourselves in. We seem to have forgotten the great achievements that were won for African American equality not so many years ago and the many lives that were lost fighting for that cause. Are our memories incapable of reaching back that far, or is it that we have failed to educate ourselves on the true meaning and purpose of enfranchisement?

Many African Americans spend a multitude of time complaining about a long list of issues and the needs of the African American community such as unemployment, education, discrimination, and criminal injustice, to name a few. These same complaining individuals are the very ones who do not partake in the political process of this great nation and are, thereby, unraveling Dr. Martin Luther King Jr.'s wonderful dream. It is imperative that we, as a people, get involved in governing ourselves and our communities so that the issues that overwhelmingly affect our people can be properly addressed. We must take responsibility for our own streets and organize ourselves with the intention of rebuilding our communities.

In this book, I will expose what I feel is the real culprit responsible for the seemingly never-ending disparities affecting the African American community. I feel that not enough people in the African American community recognize the debilitating effects of a culture that glorifies lawlessness and promotes a sense of inferiority. Why do we, as African Americans, allow our communities to remain in a state of poverty and disarray? Is it because we, as a people, are inferior to other ethnic groups and do not possess the intelligence required to solve the problems that plague our communities? Will we, as a people, ever emerge from the depths of the economic abyss? Will we ever become a political force to be reckoned with? These are all questions that I will attempt to provide answers to. The answers to these questions are not as complex as many may think. If we take a long look at ourselves and our neighborhoods, we may find real solutions that will solve our real problems!

CHAPTER 1

A Permanent Underclass

The inner cities of America have remained uninspired and under-developed for so long that they have developed a seemingly permanent sense of despair. The persistence of serious social problems in inner-city areas have helped to perpetuate negative images of African Americans and have contributed to the increasing polarization of American social and political life along racial lines. Many African Americans continue to attribute the problems of the inner city to racism, which is still partially true. Racism and White suburban flight from urban areas have left cities across America coping with high crime rates, high poverty rates, and low educational attainment. Racism is not a thing of the past; however, the White man is not the enemy anymore!

Ignorance is the enemy of the African American community, and it is high time for us to stomp out this ugly enemy. Ignorance can be blamed for many of the ills that plague the African American community. Ignorance of the political process has led to widespread political apathy and a lack of representation in public office that results in a lack of consideration of African American issues when making policy decisions. For far too long, our communities have been ignored and neglected. African American neighborhoods have been allowed to become dilapidated, crime-ridden, drug-infested areas of low economic value. This is not the result of African Americans choosing not to vote but rather their choosing to vote for politicians who do nothing for them. We should be independent voters, willing to vote for candidates from either party, depending on which side has our best interest at heart. We should stop voting solely for the Democratic party.

African Americans are the most loyal bloc of Liberal voters. An overwhelming majority of African Americans vote for Liberals in almost every election, both state/local and presidential. Many do so instinctively as if that is the only choice they have. A round 80 to 90 percent of African Americans identify as Democrats, whether they are ideologically conservative, moderate, or liberal (White and Laird 2020).

Ismail White and Chryl Laird argue that African Americans vote as a unified group because of slavery and segregation. Strong social bonds were needed for survival and resistance to oppression. The social experience of African Americans dictates their political choices. African American voters are expected to follow the lead of the group. We are influenced by the social expectations of other African Americans. Voting for someone who will represent you is an especially important decision that should be made by considering what is best for you as an individual and your family first, then what is best for your community, second. It seems that African American voters vote as a bloc, pledging allegiance to the Liberal party regardless of their level of education, economic status, religious preference, or what type of neighborhood they live in. This cohesiveness would be a good thing if it were used to better serve the Black community. We vote together, but that is about all we do together. We are not all the same and are no longer having to stand together to fight oppression and overt racism, so why do we feel the need to vote the same? We should, as a group, vote for who will better serve our interests.

The Liberal party has failed to serve us in a manner that is conducive to the survival and growth of our neighborhoods; therefore, we should consider voting for whatever party will better serve us. By serving us, I do not mean give us free stuff. Yes, I said it and I will say it again! African Americans should consider voting for conservative candidates if those candidates will better serve the economic needs and interests of our communities. It would not be the first time African Americans aligned themselves with the party of Abraham Lincoln. When the freedman first gained the vote, they voted for Republicans against the segregationist policies of southern Democrats. It was not until Franklin Roosevelt's New Deal and Harry Truman's executive orders to desegregate the military and end discrimination in federal employment did African Americans switch over and vote for Democrats because it benefited them to do so. We need to force both parties to compete for our votes to get more of what we need no matter which party is in power.

The economic and social policies of Liberals, although seemingly well intended, have had an adverse effect on the very people they were designed to help. Social welfare programs such as food stamps, section 8 housing vouchers, Medicaid, free school lunch, and the Special Supplemental Nutrition Program for Women, Infants, and Children (WIC) have crossed the line of providing help to completely discouraging individual initiative, accountability, and self-improvement. I consider these programs to be the number one factor in the perpetuation of African Americans being trapped in poverty. This is mainly due to their own ignorance and failure to understand what is really taking place. The recipients have become handicapped by government handouts and accustomed to pity and preferential treatment. The government cannot and should not take the place of family. The benefits of hard work will always be better for families than the limited benefits of government assistance. Welfare is not good enough for any family. Black families must take charge of their own lives and realize that they are capable and responsible for uplifting themselves. There is dignity in work, no matter the type of work you perform. Economic self-sufficiency comes through employment, and family stability results from personal responsibility.

Are we political chumps? Why is the African American community still committed to the Democratic party? Why is such a large percentage of the African American population underemployed, miseducated, on welfare, or in prison? Why do so many of our young men choose to be drug dealers rather than legal business

3

owners? As Malcolm X once said, "You put the Democrats first and the Democrats put you last." It is no coincidence that so many of our people are on welfare, in prison, or living in government housing (section 8). It is no coincidence that we have more young men choosing to become drug dealers than legal business owners in Black neighborhoods. When we vote, we vote for Liberals in hopes that they will help our people, but it seems that we might fare better without their kind of "help." It is time to wake up! The enemy is not who you think they are!

Black America as a solid unit held together by the common cause of fighting oppression no longer exists because the war is over. We have lost the war but have won many individual battles. There is no longer a war raging against White oppressors doing everything in their power to discriminate against African Americans, but instead, we are fighting a new war—the war to end the African American poverty cycle that is perpetuated by our political and economic ignorance and the misguided intentions of Liberal policies that are making it harder for African Americans to succeed. During the civil rights era, there was a need for larger-than-life leaders and a "Black Agenda" that gave us direction on as to what we should be fighting for, when and where those battles would take place, and how we were to go about fighting those battles. Today, after desegregation, affirmative action, urban decay, and globalization have splintered the African American population, there is no real common ground among African Americans other than our African ancestry.

During segregation, African Americans had no choice but to create their own businesses and support those businesses that were confined to the boundaries of their neighborhoods. Because African Americans were not allowed to live among Whites, eat in White restaurants, or attend White schools, they created their own self-sufficient communities that did not rely on outside support to survive. As my mother would say, "People want what they can't have." That saying holds true with African Americans who began to give their patronage to businesses owned by Whites and other ethnic groups once segregation ended. African American-owned businesses such as restaurants, banks, grocery stores, clothing stores, and even theaters, when combined, supported the African American culture and sense of pride began to disappear as a result. Legislative policies designed to bring about equality between the races have not been allowed to work as they should because of the White backlash that attempted to thwart each one. Whites fought, and in subtle ways continue to fight, to impede African American success. This has led to the limited success of desegregation as a social revolution.

After the Civil War ended, the nearly four million freed slaves found themselves free from bondage and enslaved by a new type of slavery. Planters, who dominated the South economically and politically, fought to maintain control and moved quickly to prevent the freedmen from obtaining land, equal protection under the law, and political equality. The former Confederate States began to pass a series of laws known as the black codes, designed to reduce the newly gained rights of African Americans down to basically none besides the right to marry, enter contracts, own property, and testify against other African Americans in a court of law. Black codes specified that African Americans could only work in certain occupations, low-paying ones usually, and placed limits on them owning property. As a result of these codes, African Americans found themselves working for Whites in conditions like slavery.

It has been sixty-six years since the reversal of the *Plessy v. Ferguson* decision on May 17, 1954, which ended the era of government-sanctioned segregation. Since then, the United States has become an integrated society where it is no longer publicly contested that people of all races are inherently equal and entitled to full privileges of citizenship. Although the law provides for a fully integrated and equal society, the reality is that America is still largely racially segregated and divided by economics. Although African Americans are doing much better today as compared to the years before the end of segregation, there still exists a large economic gap between African Americans and White Americans. African Americans are still twice as likely to be unemployed or hold low paying jobs with less benefits, if any at all. On average, African American households earn about 64 percent of what White households earn, and African American median wealth is about 16 percent that of Whites. There are large

5

disparities in educational attainment as well. What is the cause of these persistent disparities? America is far from perfect, yet she has become the integrated, equal opportunity nation that Dr. MLK Jr. envisioned. With that being the case, why are we still having to have conversations about the educational disparities affecting the African American community?

In the last twenty years, the White student population in Bibb County, Georgia public schools has steadily dropped. During the same time, the Black student population has remained roughly the same. As of the 2022–2023 school year, Bibb County public schools had a total enrollment of 21,392 students, a five-year high (Corley, 2022). Around 16,600 of those students are Blacks; 2,593 Whites; 1,238 Hispanics; 627 identifying as two or more races; 281 Asians; and 28 American Indians (Public School Review, 2022). These numbers show a steady withdrawal of White students from Bibb County public schools, as there were 24,840 students enrolled in 1996, with 16,680 students being Black and 7,829 of them being White (Blankenship a nd Ragusea, 2017). The racial distribution within the schools has changed tremendously as well.

Take Central High School, for example; when I attended Central in the late '90s and early 2000s, the racial makeup was close to what it was in 1996 with 58.5 percent of the student population being Black and 41.4 percent being White. As of 2016, the population of Central High School was 92.6 percent Black and 7.3 percent White. The 2017–2018 enrollment data showed that there were fifteen schools in Bibb County that are listed as all-Black schools. That number represents 40 percent of the schools in Bibb County. That number has also increased from 27.5 percent of the schools being all-Black in 1996.

These numbers left me curious as to where all the White students have gone. Other historians have researched this issue in all its complexity. They give excellent background information leading to the current discussion, such as pointing out the fact that Southern leaders intentionally did little to integrate the schools despite it being made law. Some of them make the claim that "White flight" is not the culprit behind increasing school segregation. They claim that the cause of the declining percentage of White students in public schools across the South are due to a declining White birth rate. I disagree with them, and I believe that the resegregation of Bibb's public schools is the result of White flight from the inner-city neighborhoods into the suburbs, thereby creating less racially diverse neighborhoods and less racially diverse schools. I will attempt to explain not only where the White students have gone but also why they continue to leave (Blankenship and Ragusea, 2017).

On Monday, May 17, 1954, Middle Georgia educators received a shock that many had never expected in their lifetimes. The US Supreme Court outlawed segregation in public schools in a sweeping decision. Dr. Mark A. Smith, superintendent of schools at that time, was quoted to have said, "We will just have to cross that bridge when we come to it." He was one of the twenty-one members of the Georgia Education Commission who had been called into immediate session to discuss "a program to insure continued and permanent segregation of the races" (*The Macon Telegraph*, 1954). School superintendents, boards of education, and teachers all began holding special meetings the same night the Supreme Court decision came down to begin finding ways to deal with the ruling. Superintendents of surrounding counties felt that there would be no desegregation because as A. T. Wimberly, superintendent of Twiggs County schools, put it, "The Negroes don't want it [mixed schools]." L. H. Henderson, chairman of the Toombs County Board of Education, was quoted having said "there will be a wholesale killing down here" in response to the desegregation ruling (*The Macon Telegraph*, 1954).

Another ten years would pass before any real action would be taken to desegregate public schools in Bibb County. It would not be until July 2, 1964, the day the Civil Rights Act of 1964 was enacted. This new piece of legislation would force desegregation of not only public schools but would also desegregate all public accommodations such as restaurants, hotels, water fountains, and outlawed the separate waiting rooms and seating areas of theaters and hospital wards. It did so by authorizing the US attorney general to bring lawsuits against school districts that continued to resist desegregation laws. Progress was being made in a lot of areas, but many school districts were still dragging their feet on desegregation and using all sorts of delay tactics to keep pushing it further down the road. Finally, on May 27, 1968, the Supreme Court handed down their ruling on the *Green v. County School Board of New Kent County, Virginia*, which set specific factors that must be addressed by school districts converting to a unitary system, forcing stubborn hold-out school districts to convert or lose federal funding.

By August 1971, Bibb County public high schools and middle schools were desegregated, and the school district was no longer engaging in any intentional discrimination with respect to the assignment of students to the middle and high schools. By the 1980s, integration of Bibb's public schools was no longer an issue, and on Tuesday, March 20, 2007, US District Judge Wilbur D. Owens Jr. declared the Bibb County school system a unitary system, having met all court obligations to fully integrate its schools into one system, and released it from a desegregation order after decades of court supervision. "This order is an affirmation that the school district has operated in compliance with the longstanding desegregation decree," said Bibb County School Superintendent Sharon Patterson (*The Telegraph*, 2007).

It would seem to most people in America today that we now live, work, and go to school in an integrated society, but in Bibb County, this is not quite true. Most neighborhoods here are still separated by race. Racial segregation is also associated with economic segregation. As desegregation laws were passed, Blacks who could afford to move into White neighborhoods did so. The ones who could not were left behind to live in neglected neighborhoods and to send their children to neglected, underperforming schools. When Blacks began moving in, the prejudiced Whites began moving out. As the number of Black families moving into once all-White neighborhoods within Macon continued to grow, so did the number of Black children who began to attend once all-White schools. Since the 1954 *Brown v. Board Decision*, White Maconites had begun sending their children to the newly invented segregation academies, more commonly called private schools, to avoid having them sit next to Black children in the classroom. Now that Blacks were moving into their neighborhoods, that meant they (Whites) would have to move to more secluded areas to maintain the racial separation they so desired. Since they could no longer redraw school district lines to suit their desires, they would have to create their own schools, schools that require tuition payment. They would set the tuition high enough to keep most Blacks from even thinking about sending their children there.

As the Bibb County school system worked to fully desegregate its schools in compliance with federal court order, prejudiced Whites continued to move out of Macon and into the county areas, and when that was not far enough, they moved to Monroe County, Jones County, and Crawford County where they could maintain mostly White, if not all-White, neighborhoods. Private schools were the answer to court-ordered desegregation and continue to provide Whites here in Bibb County with an alternative to sending their children to school with culturally different children, whether they be Black, poor, or, what is often the case here, Black and poor. This selfish thinking on the part of middle-class Whites caused a large drop in enrollment in Bibb schools, and that drop, in turn, caused a large drop in funding for Bibb's public schools.

"Damn the school system's well-being if White children were forced to go to school with Black children," seemed to be the sentiment of Whites who live and work in Bibb County but send their children to private schools. Only the Whites who cannot afford private school tuition send their children to public school. I have come to this conclusion based upon numbers and attitudes. The number of private schools and the percentage of the White school-aged population attending private schools is phenomenal.

As of 2021, there were twenty-two private schools in Bibb County, with roughly three thousand students enrolled. The largest of them are Stratford Academy, Mount de Sales, Tattnall Square Academy, and First Presbyterian Day School. At First Presbyterian Day School, about 87 p ercent of its students were White, 7 percent Black, 4 percent Asian, and fewer than 1 percent multiracial. At Mount de Sales Academy, about 62 percent of the students were White, 23 percent Black, 6 percent Hispanic, 7 percent Asian, and 2 percent multiracial. At Stratford Academy, about 79 percent of the students were White, 12 percent Asian, 6 percent Black, 2 percent multiracial, and fewer than 1 percent Hispanic. At Tattnall Square Academy, about 90 percent of the students were White, 5 percent Black, 3 percent Asian, and fewer than 1 percent multiracial and American Indian (Corley, 2021).

According to the Georgia Department of Education's 2008 statistics, the White population of Bibb County accounted for 47.2 percent of the overall population, yet only 22 percent of their children attend Bibb County public schools. The Black population accounted for 50.4 percent of the overall population, and 73 percent of their children attended Bibb's public schools (Georgia Department of Education, 2008). White Maconites began to pull their children out of the Bibb public school system in 1954 following *Brown v. Board* and took part in the mass exodus of roughly three hundred thousand White students from public schools across the South in 1969 following the *Green v. County School Board of New Kent County, Virginia* on May 27, 1968. About two hundred private schools were formed across the South between 1954 and 1967.

When I attended one of the forums held by Mercer University's Center for Collaborative Journalism on the issue of segregated schools here in Macon, the question of why so many White parents decide to send their children to private schools came up. Most of the answers that were given by those brave enough to stand up and voice their opinion mentioned something about Bibb County schools not meeting their expectations as far as curriculum, and a few more honest parents cited their Christian values and discipline problems of schools with large Black populations as the reason behind their choice. They are choosing to create and privately fund their own White school system instead of supporting integration and tolerating the large number of Black youths who do not take education seriously. They are condemning public schools for problems associated with failing school districts across the nation, and I cannot say that I blame them. When their families pulled out, the public schools lost a tremendous amount of funding that kept their segregated White schools so nice over the years. The lack of funding has, over time, created a school system with dilapidated conditions that led to mediocrity, apathy, and low expectations.

CHAPTER 2

Education Disparities

Today, schools are no longer segregated by Jim Crow laws, but they are, in fact, still segregated due to segregated neighborhoods. These segregated neighborhoods are the result of economic disparities between African Americans and Whites. Schools in areas of concentrated poverty are often failing schools with high dropout rates and low graduation rates. Schools on the other side of town in the more affluent, mostly White, areas are the complete opposite, most of the time. The socioeconomic status of the majority of Black America has not improved very much since the civil rights era, and what little money that was flowing within African American communities is now being spent elsewhere in White-owned businesses or in businesses owned by foreigners who have set up shop in the African American neighborhood but do not put money back into the African American neighborhood. The lack of investment in African American neighborhoods has caused them to become downtrodden and has a direct effect on the quality of the schools in African American neighborhoods.

Public schools in America are financed by local property taxes. This means that schools that are in areas with low real estate values have less money to spend on students than schools located in the more well-to-do neighborhoods with higher real estate values. This is called *funding segregation*. The question we need to be asking now is whether funding remains the problem after years of Title I funding, designed to provide supplemental funds to school districts that serve impoverished communities so they can meet the same educational goals as schools not located in poor communities. How much money does it take to erase the educational disparities plaguing African Americans? Is poverty the cause of the persistent educational attainment gap? Or is it a culture that does not value education?

Historically, funding segregation has contributed to school inequality. Naturally, the lesser the money a school receives, the more likely it is to have lower-paid teachers, overcrowded classrooms, older books, fewer extracurricular activities, a need for repair, and less access to social support services. Each one of these factors perpetuates inequalities between African American and White students, thereby Black and White America. Separated schools impose a heavy burden on society. African American public school students attend neighborhood schools that are predominantly African American. This trend is no coincidence; this resegregation of American schools is the result of White flight from the inner-city and the public school system.

I believe that economic segregation is the result of the Black-White educational achievement gap. Along with it comes the high financial costs of educating minority students in a high poverty context. The result is a never-ending war on poverty that all-American society will ultimately pay for. Those who fail to take advantage of educational opportunities become the burden of those who do. If African American children continue to be undereducated in segregated schools, what will become of the future adult workforce? Economically segregated communities and schools are doing a disservice to many African American children that prevents a large number of them from obtaining a world-class education, and many of them may never reach their full potential due to the negative attitudes and behavior problems caused by social tensions in the African American ghettos.

The African American ghetto is a peculiar American institution, just as slavery was between the sixteenth and nineteenth centuries. African Americans are the only people in America who have been relegated to live in and have continued to live in ghetto conditions where they are hypersegregated. The Black ghetto is the product of public policies made in the 1930s that encouraged institutional discrimination. The Federal Housing Administration implemented racially restrictive covenants that ensured that most African Americans would be denied the option of obtaining FHA-backed mortgages, effectively preventing them from pursuing the American dream of home ownership.

African Americans were forced to live in neighborhoods with high concentrations of poverty by three specific public policies. The urban renewal program that began in 1949 and removed African American populations out of the areas that Whites deemed to be desirable to more marginal neighborhoods. Then came the Federal-Aid Highway Act of 1956. This program broke up and destroyed mostly African American neighborhoods and created physical barriers of isolation that made African Americans even more marginalized and separated. The third was a federally sponsored public housing program of the 1950s and 1960s that herded African American public housing residents into buildings and neighborhoods where everyone around them was also poor. White public housing residents were not treated in this same manner. The creation of the Black ghetto was fueled by racial discrimination and designed to subordinate Black Americans during the Civil Rights Movement as Blacks began to demand equality.

Obviously, there are some leftover hard questions from the Civil Rights Movement. What do we do about the disparities that still exist? The first step is to acknowledge, as a society, that these disparities persist because of indolence; second, place the blame on the responsible parties; and third, enact education and welfare reform that will incentivize diligence, hard work, and self-development. We must pick up where the Civil Rights Movement left off. The Civil Rights Movement ended in 1968 after the passage of the Civil Rights Act of 1964, the Voting Rights Act of 1965, and the Fair Housing Act of 1968. The movement was successful at eliminating overt discrimination based on race, ethnicity, national origin, or religion by governments, government-funded institutions, and private individuals affecting interstate commerce. Racial discrimination in housing, education, employment, public accommodations, transportation, and voting were all made illegal by these legislative acts. However, it must be pointed out that there is still plenty of work that must be done. The work of civil rights leaders fought discrimination against the African American community and brought about Black solidarity. What their work did not do was ensure that Black America understood the importance of self-development and of the necessity of being prepared for the new opportunities being afforded to them.

Are low education achievement levels of African Americans caused by poverty? It is my opinion that this explanation is partially correct. A poverty mindset is to blame for the lack of educational achievement by African American children. Black poverty is an issue that needs to become the focus of governmental action very soon, not in the form of more government assistance but in the form of welfare and education reform. An overly supportive welfare system is inadvertently crippling low-income African Americans, thereby preventing them from rising into the middle class. Well-intentioned governmental welfare programs that were designed to help African Americans have hindered the self-development that is necessary for socioeconomic advancement. Racism is not preventing us from achieving socioeconomic advancement. Racism in systems still exists; however, it can be overcome.

African Americans are resilient. We have overcome close to four hundred years of chattel slavery and oppression in this country, and we can overcome anything. After all, this is America, the land of opportunity. African Americans have gone from being slaves and servants to become the driving force behind popular culture in America. There are thousands of examples of people who have come from an impoverished background and have taken advantage of a free public school education to become successful and productive members of society. There are opportunities available to all citizens of this nation regardless of race, creed, color, or what neighborhood you grew up in. There are those who claim that the lack of educational achievement of many African American children follows from the extraordinary rates of poverty within the African American community and the astounding rate of which African American men are incarcerated. While this holds true, in my opinion, for some, it does not explain the situation for all.

A lack of education leads to the mass imprisonment of African American males, rendering them incapable of contributing to the lives of their children and keeping them from living in poverty. If the fathers are uneducated and are incarcerated because of that fact, then what led to the father's low educational achievement? If the same holds true for their grandfathers having been absent from the home due to a lack of education and subsequent incarceration, what led to the grandfather's low educational achievement? The environment in which impoverished children live seems to be the culprit here. Generation after generation of African American males do not end up in prison, sometimes in the same prison together, solely because their fathers were absent. There is a way out of the cycle. The question is why don't more young African American males who are placed on the highway of poverty exit off onto the road to success? I believe the answer lies within the culture of Black America.

While it is the responsibility of a school board to ensure that all students in all the schools under their authority receive the same rigorous education and be given ample opportunity to graduate on time and be college ready, it is the responsibility of African American parents to make sure that their children's schools are equipped adequately with every resource necessary to graduate college-or-career-ready students and to instill in them the work ethic required to succeed in school. We, as African Americans, must take more responsibility for our neighborhoods and our schools. Ineffective schools fail students and the entire community that they serve and contribute to high incarceration rates of young Black men and the cycle of poverty. This is where the concept of Black nationalism comes into play.

It is time for us to start taking pride in our neighborhoods and come together in unity to rebuild our communities. It is time for us to set an example, for our youth to follow, of a strong, thriving community of law-abiding citizens who are politically active and concern themselves with the ownership of African American communities. It is time we stand up for higher educational attainment for Black students, especially Black male students. It is no one's responsibility except ours to teach Black male students to pull their pants up and get their grades up to par so that they can fully realize their potential to be great. It is time to put a stop to this ignorant rap music culture that has taken control of many of our young Black men and influenced them to engage in street gang activity and other illegal activities to gain "street credibility," something that is not tangible.

I am not against rap music, but I am against ignorant rap music that perpetuates violence, drug activity, and other behaviors that turn our young African American men into stereotypes who become convicted felons instead of college graduates. We must make them into men before the justice system turns them into caged animals. It is imperative that we keep young Black males out of cages and in African American communities so that they can become providers for their families and raise their sons to be men who will do the same. The education of African American students should include teaching them their rightful place in American society to dispel the ignorant view of gaining education as acting White and dumbing yourself down, making you Blacker and cooler.

Where there is a will, there is a way! Research by Rice University's Kinder Institute for Urban Research shows that African Americans are most likely to value a postsecondary education in becoming successful. We, as a people, value education and want the best possible education for our children. The problem is that we do not stand together as a united, powerful force to make changes to the culture, governance, curriculum, instruction, policy, and the lack of parental involvement that are creating problems in majority Black schools and school districts. We need to hold community meetings to address the concerns of parents and issues that African American students are facing and then take these issues and concerns to the school boards, who should be happy to hear from African American parents and students on how to better serve African American parents and students. That should make their job a little easier, getting answers and feedback from the people whom they serve rather than resulting to trial and error. The key is that we, as African Americans, must make our collective voice heard rather than continue to complain behind closed doors.

While poverty and the lack of complete families play a major role in the low educational achievement of African American students, a lack of discipline and proper social behavior plays an even greater role. Proper social behavior? What is proper social behavior for Black students in America? And who determines what is and what isn't proper social behavior? Are there a set of universal social norms that all cultures worldwide can agree upon? Maybe. Maybe not. But in America, we do have a set of acceptable social behaviors that can and do apply to all people who live in or visit this country.

All schoolteachers, both Black and White, who teach in both urban and rural areas, are trained in classroom management. Classroom management incorporates certain standards or norms that are to be adhered to create and maintain an effective learning environment. Students are compelled to abide by certain class rules for the benefit of themselves and other students. The better each student behaves, the better each student will be. Well-behaved students make greater academic progress than students who do not practice proper social behavior. Proper social behavior seems to be the key to academic success. Are these behaviors first introduced to children when they enter kindergarten? We should hope not! Children should be introduced to acceptable social behaviors long before they enter school. The problem is that acceptable social behaviors differ greatly based upon family background and culture.

Family background and culture ultimately impact the academic achievement of students and largely contribute to the achievement gap that exists between races. This is because a student's family background and culture shape their perceptions and expectations of education. Children from different backgrounds enter school at different levels of readiness. Parental involvement in a child's development has an especially important impact on the level of educational achievement of Black children. Differences in parenting styles impact a child's understanding of social behavior and future educational achievement.

In her book, *Unequal Childhoods*, sociologist Annette Lareau argues that there are two main types of parenting: concerted cultivation and the achievement of natural growth.

Concerted cultivation is normally practiced by parents of middle-class status, both Black and White. These types of parents are more likely to involve themselves in their child's education. They get their children involved in extracurricular activities or sports, and they teach their children proper social behaviors, such as good communication skills that act as a form of social capital that will enable them to effectively communicate their needs and negotiate with authority figures throughout their lives. The achievement of natural growth, on the other hand, is generally practiced by poor and working-class families. These types of parents do not play a large role in their children's education, and their children are less likely to participate in extracurricular activities or play sports. Missing out on these things puts their children at a disadvantage because they do not learn the same social behaviors that middle- and upper-class children do.

These children from poor and working-class Black families face language barriers and differences in social and cultural norms in interactions and learning styles. They have low levels of receptiveness of their culture to White American culture and low levels, if any at all, of acceptance of the White American culture. African American students from high poverty areas do not align themselves with mainstream (White) cultural views as easily as middle- and upper-class Black students do and consequently have a harder time in school. African American students should be able to embrace their own culture and, at the same time, learn how to survive in American society.

Since we do not have full ownership of our communities, we are forced to assimilate into the mainstream (White) culture of America. We have no other choice until we begin to work together to rebuild our communities and take back ownership of and responsibility for the schools, businesses, crimes, and poverty in our neighborhoods. Until we do this, we will continue to face disproportionate levels of poverty, unemployment, incarceration, racial profiling, and police brutality by White police officers who feel that it is their duty to keep Black people in line and force us to assimilate.

Assimilate or be poor is the reality for people of African descent in America. We now stand poised in a position to teach our Black students the value of education and the social skills that will keep them out of harm's way and enable them to reach their full academic potential. We need to inspire every Black student that we encounter to place more emphasis on his or her education. We need to promote the idea of being studious as being Black and pursuing higher levels of education as being Blacker and cooler.

Rebuilding our downtrodden neighborhoods through political action that will give a real voice to our concerns and forming neighborhood coalitions focused on improving our socioeconomic status and the attitudes of the children about performing well in school will increase the academic performance of African American students and ultimately reduce poverty within the African American community. What we must realize is that we cannot continue to blame racism and funding segregation for the low achievement of African American students.

Historically, public schools were financed solely by local property taxes. Schools that were in areas with low real estate values had less money to spend on students than schools located in the more well-to-do neighborhoods with higher real estate values. In most major cities, African American students are normally the ones who live in neighborhoods with lower property values and, therefore, were more likely to receive lower funding at their schools. The lesser money a school receives, the more likely it is to have lower-paid teachers, overcrowded classrooms, older books, fewer extracurricular activities, and less access to social support services. Each one of these factors perpetuates inequalities between Black and White students.

Today, we cannot continue to blame a lack of funding for the achievement gap between Black and White students. The Title I federal aid program provides funds to schools with high percentages of low-income students. These funds help provide the social support services for at-risk youth that they would not receive otherwise. Living in a community with economic and social inequalities contributes to negative attitudes and behavior problems due to social tensions. These negative attitudes rather than a perceived lack of funding are the cause of the persistent educational disparities, which, in turn, are the cause of the persistent economic disparities effecting the African American community.

Once we rebuild our neighborhoods, we will gain more social cohesiveness, which will, in turn, create greater college aspirations among African American students. It is imperative that we do so because being born into a family living in a low socioeconomic area can have negative effects on a child's educational achievement long before starting school. African American students are, on average, one year behind in vocabulary and math skills when they first enter kindergarten. This achievement gap impacts the upward mobility of Black students. Not only does it have negative effects on them, but it also effects American society in relation to the quality of our work-force and the competitiveness in an increasingly globalized economy.

Our economy has shifted away from blue-collar manufacturing and turned into a knowledge-based, technology-driven economy in which education has become the most important factor to achieving success and prosperity. Having a strong education will not only pre-pare Black students for the workforce, but it will also enable them to attain and maintain careers that will break the cycle of poverty for them and their offspring. Lower-achieving students are more likely to drop out of high school and, for the ones who decide not to involve themselves in criminal activity, will be forced to work jobs that only require minimal training and skills. These jobs pay much less than those requiring more education and make it extremely hard, if not impossible, to become successful and prosperous. Therefore, it is of the utmost importance that we, as the African American community, work to reduce and eventually eliminate the racial achievement gap. Doing so will eliminate economic disparities and help to rebuild our communities.

According to the Alliance for Excellent Education, $310 billion would be added to the US economy by 2020 if minority students graduated at the same rate as White students. It has been reported by the United States Census Bureau that the median income of White families is $62,545 while the median income for Black families is $38,409. The median income for Hispanic families is $ 39,730 and

$75,027 is the median income of Asian families. The difference in these income levels has a direct correlation to educational opportunities made available and taken advantage of by the various groups. When a Black student drops out of high school, they will experience a high level of difficulty in finding a stable, decent-paying job. On average, young adults who drop out of high school will only make about $21,000 annually, whereas high school graduates will earn about $30,000 annually. The high school graduate will earn $630,000 more during their life. Black students who do not attend college due to complications caused by the racial achievement gap miss out on over $450,000 in lifetime earnings. I think the message hear is noticeably clear: Black students must go to college, our communities need Black students to go to college, and America needs Black students to go to college.

America needs educated young Black people who can fight and destroy the stereotype threat that many of them, young Black males especially, face today. This stereotype threat both perpetuates and is caused by the achievement gap (Aronson 2004). Students who are not expected to do well demonstrate low expectations for themselves and self-handicapping tendencies (Zuckerman, Kieffer, and Knee 1998). Stereotypes are powerful and can threaten how students evaluate themselves. When a Black male student, no matter how intelligent, recognizes that he is being stereotyped, his academic identity and intellectual performance become altered.

This theory was tested by psychologist Claude Steele when he gave Black and White college students a half-hour test using difficult questions from the verbal Graduate Record Examination. In the stereotype-threat condition, students were told that the test they were taking diagnosed intellectual ability. By telling them that the test would diagnose intellectual ability, it potentially elicited the stereotype that Blacks were less intelligent than Whites. In the nonstereotype-threat condition, students were told that the test they were taking was a problem-solving lab task that implied nothing about ability levels. By doing so, stereotypes became irrelevant, and the Black students performed just as well as the White students. In the beforementioned stereotype-threat condition, Black students who were evenly matched with White students in their group by SAT scores performed worse compared to the White students (Steele 2010).

Other studies conducted on the racial achievement gap show that higher socioeconomic status is correlated with higher participation in politics (Ogbu 1992). There is a lack of representation of minority groups in public office; therefore, fewer resources are effectively allocated to Black communities. African Americans who earn less money are more likely to seek less gainful employment due to lower levels of educational achievement and are less likely to participate in politics. As we know, the more education a person receives, the more likely they are to attain well-paying jobs.

There exists a disparity between the educational attainment of White Americans and Black Americans. Less than 30 percent of bachelor's degrees are awarded to Blacks (National Science Foundation's Division of Science Resources Statistics 2010). Less political activity leads to underrepresentation of Blacks in leadership which, in turn, leads to our community needs not being met by educational and social welfare policies that are implemented by government officials not in tune with the Black community. Naturally, more back representation in state and local governments as well as on school boards will lead to more consideration of Blacks and our issues when making policy decisions (Meier and England 1984).

CHAPTER 3

Hip-Hop Culture

Hip-hop has been productive as a form of revolution against systematic racism in America, but over time, it has evolved into something less productive yet more powerful than ever as it glorifies the ills of Black America. For 398 years, Black Americans have been the underclass in American society except for a minute upper class and a growing middle-class population. There are possible explanations for this, such as an unequal education that is the result of underfunded schools or the more propagated theories that rely on discrimination and years of oppression by White America. Although these theories do hold weight in this ongoing argument, they fail to expose a more deeply rooted and persistent cause of Black American inequality. The culture of Black America today is so much different from mainstream America. It is common to see things that are shocking to onlookers from other ethnic groups. Black American culture is largely centered around hip-hop culture, and hip-hop culture may be the culprit that continues to perpetuate the disparities that keep the poorest Black Americans downtrodden.

Hip-hop is not just a style of music but also a culture! It is a culture that has embraced the ideas of martyred icons such as Malcolm X, Huey P. Newton, Stokeley Carmichael, and H. Rap Brown of the Black Power Movement while at the same time rejecting the passivity of Dr. King and his dream. Hip-hop is a representation of a leaderless generation searching for new heroes. Formed in the post-civil rights era with a noticeable vacuum of leadership, the renewal of states' rights and Reaganomics, and a growing sense of abandonment among Black working-class families, hip-hop emerged as the new Black leadership. Hip-hop artists became the new revolutionaries fighting back against oppression. Chuck D of Public Enemy called his group the "Black Panthers of Rap" as they dramatized Black identity and addressed racism as a tool of the US power structure.

Chuck D, the lead vocalist of the group Public Enemy, is one of the most politically and socially conscious artists of the hip-hop generation. A by-product of the turbulent 1960s, Chuck witnessed firsthand the issues of racism and classism. He has been criticized as being an angry, militant radical for having stood up against the biased mainstream. Chuck D is a poet and philosopher who focuses on things that the Black community can do to help itself and ways people from other communities can help. In his book, *Fight the Power: Rap, Race, and Reality*, Chuck D addresses controversial issues including the role and responsibility of entertainers and celebrities, gangster rap and the current state of rap music, education, community, and economic development.

As Reagan's America became perilous to youths of color, the well-organized and well-financed right-wing backlash against Civil Rights Movement gains cut off opportunities for urban youth of color. Trickle-down economics starved local governments of the necessary revenue needed to maintain the effectiveness of social programs designed to assist the poor and lower working-class. This combined with local taxpayer revolts led to massive White flight, suburban sprawl, and racial resegregation. After two decades of progress in integration, Black Americans were succumbing to conditions of increased racial and economic isolation. Those who were not prepared to take advantage of the opportunities afforded by the passing of the Civil Rights Acts and Affirmative Action were left behind in the Black neighborhoods that would quickly turn into ghettos once all the middle-class Black folks moved out, headed for suburbia.

Those abandoned Black communities would become permanently locked into poverty and joblessness.

As the Black community awaited a new Black Moses to come and deliver them into the promised land, the hip-hop generation was coming of age and along with them came a new revolutionary consciousness. Public Enemy stepped into the void along with Minister Louis Farrakhan to encourage young Black men to unite and stop killing one another. A hostile climate had developed in America toward Black people and the continued struggle for economic equality.

According to Chuck D, Black culture, especially the negative aspects of it, became profitable in the 1980s, and White corporations figured out that they could take advantage of it. Because of the commercialization of negative Black imagery such as Black men being portrayed on film and on television as pimps, drug dealers, and players, fatherless Black children from impoverished neighborhoods only see Black men in a derogatory manner. Many grow up thinking that the only way for them to make money is to be a hustler.

"Many in the world of Hip-Hop have begun to believe that the only way to blow up and become megastars is by presenting themselves in a negative light." Most artists make positive tracks along with the more gutter tracks, but it is mostly the gutter tracks that receive the attention. "That's what I feel happened with Tupac. Tupac had a loyalty to Black people without a doubt. His early albums sound like a combination of Public Enemy and N.W.A. Tupac found that when he said things that were pro-Black and militant, people were not paying any attention to what he was saying so he decided to go more into the side of darkness, like Bishop, the character he played in the movie *Juice*. The more he played the 'bad boy' or 'rude boy' image, the bigger and bigger he got" (*Fight the Power: Rap, Race, and Reality*, 3).

Tupac used gangster imagery to reach young Black males and deliver a message to us in a way only another young Black male could. The negative imagery often overshadows the positive message being delivered below the surface. This combined with the harshness of impoverished neighborhoods and derogatory programming on television have led to a point where life imitates art. "It's such a serious issue because the derogatory programming leads to a point where life imitates art, and a blur develops between fantasy and reality. I believe that television is one of the main reasons for the criminal mindedness of Black youth" (*Fight the Power: Rap, Race, and Reality*, 6).

Chuck D speaks about how drugs and alcohol have had negative effects on the Black community. Drug use has become a normal part of everyday life in the hood. It has been accepted by many as a part of the Black culture. He is correct in citing drug culture as part of the reason for the stagnation of hip-hop as an art form and as a vehicle for change and progress in the Black community. The glorification of drug culture, the gangster rapper, and thug life have led to the war on drugs, the war on gangs, and, subsequently, the war on young Black males. These wars have deemed the young Black male as public enemy number one and brought about the oppressive crime legislation with mandatory sentences, more cops, more prisons, and less investment in urban neighborhoods.

When you show young Black men that you do not care about their lives, they begin to stop caring about their lives, and a vicious cycle of poverty and crime continue with no end in sight. Gangster rap became the vehicle used to show the world the sad conditions of the ghetto. Gangster rappers became the journalists speaking for the brothers on the corner. The gangster rapper can be a hardcore talking hero or a negative role model, and too often today, in hip-hop, the rappers are just negative role models. "We need to have more people step up and say something of substance" (Chuck 1997).

In *Fight the Power: Rap, Race, and Reality*, Chuck D describes gangster rap as one segment of rap music, which has many different segments. In my opinion, gangster rap is the packaged, marketed, and sold demise of Black America. Large corporations, for-profit prisons, and even the government at every level benefit from the cheap labor done by prisoners. Gangster rap glorifies gang life and behavior, perpetuating the violence and drug culture in the Black inner city while simultaneously serving as a means of entertainment for White kids in the suburbs. Rap music and hip-hop are often used interchangeably, although I feel that there is a difference between the two. I feel that hip-hop is meaningful poetry being rapped over a beat, whether it be jazz, rock, funk, or blues. I define rap music as less meaningful party music that glorifies the ills of the Black community to take ownership of those ills and create a sense of pride in the community even if it does not measure up to mainstream, middle-class standards and is impoverished.

He goes on to describe hip-hop as a subculture of Black culture and the result of Black creativity in the last quarter of the twentieth century. According to him, gangster rap is a legitimate art form because it talks about certain aspects of life. The term "gangster rap" was first coined by N.W.A. in the song "Gangsta, Gangsta." The song was about gang life in Los Angeles. This style of rap music tells the realities of street life; however, what it does not tell is the fact that most recording artists who consider themselves gangster rappers are not really gangsters. Chuck D believes that gangster rap should not be censored because he views it as a plea for help by those who are not represented by the mainstream. "Certain aspects of it should be commended for being informative and, until the problems in the poorer communities get fixed, certain elements of what's termed 'Gangsta Rap' will not disappear" (*Fight the Power: Rap, Race, and Reality,* 249).

Gangster rap got mainstream exposure as a problem when it began to reach White kids in the suburbs. Before that, there were no movements to censor the music when it was confined to the Black community. It only became a politically viable issue to address because of its potential to influence suburban White kids. Before that, politicians were not paying attention to the messages being delivered by journalists from the hood. Gangster rap is a sea of angry Black voices yelling and being followed by millions. In "They Don't Give a Fuck About Us," Tupac said, "While I'm kickin' rhymes, kick it to their children's minds, now they give a fuck about us."

Rap music has become a worldwide phenomenon. Rap has found its way into every region of the world. It has become representative of the young mentality and, therefore, can use its power to educate Black youth about themselves and their history and spread a positive message about being Black and intelligent. Hip-hop culture is a subculture of Black culture; therefore, it should function with the sole purpose of progressing Black people. As of now, rap music has become self-defeating; it is being created by us and used to destroy us. The negative aspects of it are being glorified and commercialized for entertainment purposes. The killing of Black people has become entertainment. Record labels are controlling our culture and pushing foolishness and garbage upon us and calling it entertainment. Negative imagery is being reinforced in the Black community from the outside and perpetuated from the inside.

Hip-hop is the music of revolution! The hip-hop generation is a generation of revolutionaries ready to be defiant at a moment's notice whenever racism or injustice rears its ugly head! The music keeps them ready! Hip-hop has the revolutionary potential to influence political engagement among young Black Americans if used in the proper manner. The problem is that positive hip-hop is all but dead, and rap is too busy reinforcing the negative stereotypes that hinder Black progress. Rap is teaching Black youth that a thuggish adversarial stance is the proper response to what is presumed to be a racist society out to get them. Black popular culture and Black attitudes have changed dramatically since the Civil Rights Movement. Hip-hop and rap draw their strength from the militantly adversarial stance toward racist American society of the Black Power Movement.

Malcolm X, the Nation of Islam, and the Black Panther Party for Self-Defense emerged with a Black ideology that embraced Black pride, strength, and authentic Black identity. The militant attitude of Malcolm X and the Black Panthers turned into a gangster mentality when the Black Power Movement began to die off with the systematic destruction of the Black Panther Party and the murder of its leaders along with other Civil Rights- and Black Power Movement leaders and activists.

Early on, hip-hop was about telling stories through a funky beat, break dancing, disc jockeys, and graffiti art. These were the elements of an inner-city revolution designed to highlight the ghetto in a positive light while calling attention to the problems within the abandoned neighborhoods. Highlighting those problems brought about a darker form of rap. Gangster rap seemed to celebrate gangs, drugs, and promiscuity as it told the stories of people in the hood that otherwise would not be heard. Celebrating these negative aspects or not, gangster rap delivers a message about ghetto life, pointing out how the environment makes the culture and then the culture changes the environment.

Hip-hop is the poetry of the streets, and its message has shifted from just explaining what is going on in the hood to justifying what is going on. The problem with justifying the gang activity, drug culture, and promiscuity is that these negative behaviors are destroying the already-struggling communities and turning the inner cities of every major city in the United States into a jungle or something like a third-world country. Hip-hop exploded into the mainstream with the invention of the music video. Rappers on MTV reinforced the negative stereotypes of young Black men in the ghetto. The more negative the song, the more popular the song would be, and the more records the artists would sell.

The militancy and nonconformity of hip-hop today is what makes it so popular. Not all hip-hop songs are negative, but the most popular artists must maintain a ghetto fabulous image to sell their music. There are positive artists in the industry who speak about social issues in an uplifting manner, but their work is often overshadowed by the less intellectual party music. There are many who defend hip-hop's violence and misogyny as a cry for help, including University of Pennsylvania Black studies professor Michael Eric Dyson.

He has written a book called *Know What I Mean? Reflections on Hip-Hop*. Dyson takes a stand for hip-hop, defending it as the art form of degraded youth that shines a bright light on their circumstances and experiences. Dyson explains in his book how the commercial explosion of hip-hop has made the art form a victim of its own success while also acknowledging the political elements of hip-hop that are often ignored. He has become known as the hip-hop intellectual because of his advocacy for increased intellectual engagement of hip-hop music, no matter how negative it may seem. He believes that there is always a meaning behind the music. I am not so sure that I agree with him on that. Some of these new artists today do not seem to have any direction, and their music loses me. I do not know what the hell they are talking about! Dyson has always supported this art form from the abandoned and interpreted it to help others understand the significance of this untamed guerilla.

Michael Eric Dyson grew up in the streets of Detroit where he was forced to confront the disadvantages that affect the lives of many Black folks. These circumstances did not break him; instead, they opened his mind to learning and taught him the importance of education. He is a living example for impoverished Black youth longing to better themselves. He is a reminder that there is a way out of the ghetto. He stands up for the poorest Black Americans, reminding the rest of the country that they too are American and deserving of the American dream. He has shown the world that hip-hop is an important arts movement created by young working-class Black people. He attempts in his book and does a wonderful job of explaining how intense poverty and deeply rooted racism as well as unemployment in this country have led to this violent, misogynistic culture that exists in America's inner cities.

Dyson forces us to take urban life seriously and not simply view young Black males standing on the corner as thugs, drug dealers, and pimps. His work puts a human face on the ghetto. His stance is at odds with many in the Black American community who feel that hip-hop has become destructive. I do not agree with Dyson on everything, but I do agree that Black children from the hood should be taught that their culture matters and that it fits into the scheme of things in the larger American society. I feel that hip-hop is a revolutionary tool that should be used to compliment educational attainment, political involvement, and activism to bring about solutions to the very real problems of ghetto America.

Hip-hop was a cry for help against oppression in the 1980s and 1990s, but today's rap is not crying out for help. It is just yelling about selling drugs, having sex, and getting money, which is hardly helping address the plight of the ghetto. During the Black Power Movement, the music was affirmative and hopeful, not filled with violence and lyrics promoting Black-on-Black crime. Gangster rap has stemmed from and perpetuated the breakdown of community norms within

America's inner-city youth. Unwilling to listen to neighborhood elders whom they see as weak and unable to lead them, young Black males join gangs looking for what was missing at home and a means of making money by any means necessary.

In the 1980s, the ghetto had become a lawless war zone, and the White man was no longer the enemy! Hip-hop is by no means responsible for the conditions of the ghetto; bad fiscal policies of the time are to blame for this. However, glorifying and glamorizing ghetto culture has made it harder for Black children born into these unfortunate circumstances to follow the traditional path to success. Not having strong role models in front of them daily and seeing criminals with pockets full of money riding in old-school cars with twenty-four-inch rims and gold chains around their necks destroy the mainstream image of what a successful person looks like. Why pay attention in school when you can make good money selling cocaine on your neighborhood streets? Education is pointless to far too many of our Black youth, especially the males.

The attitude and style expressed by hip-hop, gangster or not, is keeping Black people in the abandoned neighborhoods down. It is teaching young Black men to be confrontational, rowdy, and profane as they emulate rappers that they see in music videos and hear on the radio. These unruly mannerisms make potential employers, Black and White, wary of all young Black men and, thereby, reduces their chances of being hired and increases their chances of getting into confrontations with law enforcement, other unruly young Black males, and falling prey to gang culture and the drug game. The Black community has made too much progress since the beginning of the Civil Rights Movement to allow our youth to continue to slip into a state of decline because of the adversarial identity of hip-hop.

Hip-hop has the potential to be uplifting and make revolutionary change in the inner city despite the popular trend of glorifying ignorance. The truth is rappers are more powerful than politicians. They influence the way people walk, talk, and dress daily. What politician can do that? If used the right way in conjunction with community organizations and city officials, hip-hop can serve its original and true purpose. It can draw support from people on the outside

31

and encourage them to step into the ghetto and take an active part in rebuilding these abandoned neighborhoods.

Rappers control their lyrics, but it is the record labels and corporations that control which songs hit the airwaves. It seems that the real culprit behind this violent, misogynistic, adversarial music are the record labels that own stock in private prisons. These corporations are the driving force behind the promoting of negative music. They turn young Black male rappers into an overnight success by creating an image that reflects the worst of ghetto life and culture. This image and lifestyle are sold to the abandoned in the ghetto who are already inclined to view the world from a disenchanted perspective. The disenchanted Black youth, often lacking positive role models, gravitate toward industry-created personas and see them as role models. It is simply supply and demand! There is a demand for apathetic, anti-authority, drug-pushing music, so the music industry supplies it. They do it with no shame; after all, it is just business.

They did not create the welfare state that is holding a lot of Black people back, they are not responsible for the educational inequalities that exist in America, and they are certainly not responsible for the individual behavior of criminals, right? They may not be responsible for the disparities that affect the Black community; however, they are responsible for what they create and put out into the world. They are poisoning our youth with apathy and the glorification of ignorance. Like the title of Nas' album, *Hip-Hop is Dead*, suggests hip-hop in its best form is dead, but that does not mean it cannot be resurrected and used to help save the abandoned Black community.

CHAPTER 4

Follow the Rules or
Play the Victim

Black America has transformed over the last five decades into what Eugene Robinson, in his book, *Disintegration: The Splintering of Black America*, describes as four distinct Black Americas separated by demography, geography, and psychology. These are the four Black Americas in existence today, according to Robinson:

- The mainstream middle-class majority with a full owner-ship stake in American society.
- The large, abandoned minority with less hope of escaping poverty and dysfunction than at any time since Reconstruction.
- The small transcendent elite with enormous wealth, power, and influence.
- The two newly emergent groups—individuals of mixed-race heritage and recent Black immigrants who brought with them a different perspective on "being Black."

Each of these four groups have different profiles, mindsets, and approaches to life. The only time, I think, members of these four distinct Black Americas come together is during worship service in the numerous churches located in Black neighborhoods. The mainstream Black folks drive from the suburbs into the inner city to attend church. They make sure they lock the doors of their BMWs or their Mercedes-Benzes on their way to the church because they are aware of the crime rates that exist in Black neighborhoods. These mainstream Black folks remain loyal to the churches they grew up in as children long after they move out of the neighborhood where the church is located. They give their money to the church but have no interest in giving a helping hand to the surrounding community. Why is that?

Civil rights laws did what they were intended to: they banned discrimination in education, housing, and employment. Affirmative action offered life-changing opportunities to those prepared to take advantage. As a result, millions of African Americans were able to climb the economic ladder and join the middle class. The poverty rate for African Americans fell steadily until the mid-1990s when it stalled around 25 percent. In 2018, the African American poverty rate was 20.8 percent. That equates to 8.9 million African Americans living below the poverty line. The White poverty rate for that same year was 8.1 percent, about 15.7 million White people living below the poverty line. I think it is important to put statistics in proper perspective so they may be understood and used in a factual manner. So about 80 percent of African Americans do not live in poverty versus 92 percent of Whites. That means that a significant number of African Americans are still living in poverty, but most of us are not, and that is something to be proud of.

The number of African Americans who cross into the middle class continues to rise. In 1967, only one in every ten African American households earned $50,000 a year. Today, that number has tripled. Forty years ago, not even two African American households, in a hundred, earned what was then the equivalent to $100,000 a year. Now one in every ten African American households belong to the upper middle class. Black America combined controls about $1 trillion a year in purchasing power, and most of that money is made and spent by the middle class who can improve the dilapidated Black neighborhoods but do not and will not do so because they realize that the poor Blacks who live there are not willing to take responsibility for themselves and maintain their neighborhoods. The mainstream Black folks moved away from the ghetto as soon as they could and never looked back. It is easy for the African American middle class to forget about the abandoned because they only constitute a small percentage of the African American population. Most of us are doing well, earning a living and playing by the rules. Those who choose to follow the mainstream playbook can rise out of the abandoned with education and hard work.

Mainstream African Americans live in a different world than the abandoned African Americans. We work in integrated settings where we have learned how to accept White Americans and be accepted by White Americans. We socialize in Black settings where solidarity flows from shared history and experience. We want to hear Black music, but we do not want to engage in ghetto behavior. We feel more comfortable attending Black churches as opposed to being one of the chocolate chips in a White congregation. In all their attempts to integrate with White America, the baby boomer generation has largely self-segregated themselves by wanting to live among Black people. We, the millennials, certainly do not feel the same way. We can fit in anywhere, and we do just that. We settle wherever our hearts desire. We do not make decisions about where we should live in terms of race. Our decisions are made based on affordability and convenience. Even still, wherever we settle, there is a perceived sense of being judged or being looked down upon, which fuels the desire for Black solidarity among mainstream African Americans.

Many African Americans have made their way into the middle class by taking advantage of public-school education. Civil rights leaders and activists fought for African Americans to be able to go to the schools of their choice to obtain a quality education because they understood the importance of education in America. They understood that without a solid education, one would most likely find oneself in poverty and remain in poverty. In 1967, 53.4 percent of Whites compared to only 29.5 percent of Blacks had completed high school, according to the Census Bureau. In 2008, the figures were

87.1 percent for Whites and 83 percent for Blacks. In 1967, 10.6 percent of Whites and only 4 percent of Blacks had completed four years of college. In 2008, 29.8 percent of Whites and 19.6 percent of Blacks had college degrees (US Census Bureau, Current Population Survey, 2008). For the 2011–2012 school year, African American students, nationwide, graduated at a rate of 69 percent compared to 86 percent for White students (Maciag, 2012). That 14 percent drop from 2008 is an indicator that things are moving in the wrong direction for African American students. It has been proven that education coupled with hard work can lead anyone to success in America.

Is African American mainstream success recognized on a national level? Do White people think that Black America is a hellhole with intractable problems that defy solution? Is it not apparent that there is an existence of an enormous African American mainstream who are fully integrated and assimilated into American society? Do people believe only what they see in movies and on television shows or news broadcasts that are constantly focusing on the negative stereotypes that confirm what people think that they already know about Black America? These same stereotypes stoke the flames of racial tension and lead African Americans to believe that most White people are racist and think of us as being ignorant and ghetto. There are many hardworking and well-educated Black people who do not buy into a race-based culture. We neither glorify violent behavior, nor do we condone the use of illegal drugs and gang culture. Not all Black men smoke and sell weed unbeknownst to some White drug heads desperately searching for the hookup at gas stations. Some years ago, I was asked if I had any weed to sell by a truckload of White teenagers who pulled up next to me at the gas pump. I was angered by their actions and the fact that they had the notion to believe that I, as an African American man, must have some weed to sell. What made them think that?

My father grew up during segregation and learned to live under the rule of Jim Crow in Macon, Georgia. Born in Twiggs County in 1946, he attended segregated schools and graduated from Peter G. Appling High School in 1964 during the midst of the Civil Rights Movement. My mother, on the other hand, was born in Cincinnati,

Ohio, in 1952. Jim Crow did not have a presence in Cincinnati. Although there was housing segregation, there was not the same kind of racist bigotry in place like there was in the South. She attended Aiken High School in the late '60s right alongside White students. She went on to attend Fisk University and graduate with a teaching degree. Ironically, it was harder for African American teachers to find jobs in the integrated North than it was for them to find employment in the newly desegregated South. This being the case, she moved to Perry, Georgia, where she began her teaching career close by in Bonaire and later met my father in nearby Macon, Georgia. My father, who was not afforded many opportunities, being a Black man in the 1964 Jim Crow South, joined the US Army and became a paratrooper. He served in the elite 82nd Airborne Division during Operation Power Pack, the US military intervention in the Dominican Republic in 1965. After his military service, he returned to Macon, Georgia, and later attended and graduated from Mercer University, a once segregated university.

My parents educated themselves and both worked extremely hard to see to it that my sister and I had everything we needed to be successful. We moved from the inner-city Bellevue community, which was not bad at the time and still is not especially compared to other inner-city neighborhoods, to suburban south Bibb County, where we were the only Black family in our subdivision. My sister and I attended Porter Elementary School and were the only or one of two Black children in our classrooms each year. Most of the friends we grew up with were White, prior to high school. Although we faced some racism, we easily assimilated into White society. We were both good students who excelled academically and became, for all intents and purposes, equal to the White students. We learned that the way to defeat racism and bigotry is to educate yourself and carry yourself with class, dignity, and pride. If you do that, even your biggest enemy will have to respect you. They may never like you, but they will respect you. We, the Black mainstream, have demanded and won equal rights and equal treatment by proving that we are equal in every way. We are living Dr. King's dream that we be judged by the content of our character and not by the color of our skin. So why is it that the abandoned have not learned to do the same?

When segregation ended, African Americans who were prepared to take advantage of newfound opportunities did so and moved up into the middle class. Along with better jobs came the ability to move out of Black neighborhoods and into the suburbs. When the more affluent Blacks left the Black community, the inner-city Black population became poorer and less educated. As they became less educated, they became more resentful toward mainstream America. Drug dealing and crime have taken the place of economic development in poor Black neighborhoods. Black-on-Black crime is a constant problem, poor people who are too sorry to get a job robbing other poor people who work hard for the few things they have, in the abandoned neighborhoods. Black lives matter, so they say, but the reality is that a Black man is more likely to be killed by another Black man rather than law enforcement officers. According to sociologist William Julius Wilson of Harvard University, the migration of industry from urban areas to the suburbs and beyond was the principal factor in the creation of what is called the Black underclass. With few well-paying jobs available nearby for low-skilled or entry-level workers, learning about and getting employment opportunities in the suburbs is a daunting ordeal. This may be so, but it is not an impossible one.

It can be argued that the disappearance of factory jobs and other work opportunities has helped create the situation we see today in Black communities where more children than not are being raised by single mothers. The jobless rate of Black men has not hindered them from making babies though. It has hindered them from being able to provide for those babies, however. All too often, young Black women find themselves pregnant by a Black man who either has no job or is underemployed. The fear of raising a baby on their own with little to no help from the father leads far too many young Black women to seek government assistance. There is little incentive for these women to marry the fathers of their children since the men are not likely to maintain stable employment and provide for the family as they should. Welfare programs make it easy for poor single mothers to decide what they can do as well or perhaps better, raising the children without the father. Welfare programs designed to help single mothers have unintentionally eliminated the need for two-parent households, which have always been and continue to be necessary for the best upbringing of a child.

The result has been devastating to the African American communities throughout the nation. When the government replaced the Black man as the head of the household, it destroyed the pride and the relevance of the Black man in the community. It has been said that welfare programs have created what has been coined "Project Queens" who are living in government housing and receiving food stamps, making a living off the government by continuing to have children by different men with no intention of getting off government assistance. What has been created is a playbook that works well: get pregnant, apply for WIC, have the baby, and start receiving money on their EBT card each month. The mother can then apply for section 8 housing with the local housing authority and be placed on the waiting list (because of the large number of applicants) and then receive either public housing or a housing voucher to find suitable housing within the local community. These young Black women know that having a baby will allow them to establish their own households, whether it be in a home they purchase or in a subsidized apartment.

The Black man lost his place and began to feel like he was less than nothing. A downtrodden man with little pride and respect for himself will not respect the sight, let alone the presence, of other men who look like him who he deems to be just as worthless as he feels he is. These Black men become perpetrators of Black-on-Black crime, whether it be violent crimes or property crimes that land them behind locked doors in a prison or displayed as an image on a rest in peace (RIP) T-shirt. Around 54 percent of all Black children are being raised in single-parent households, and in most cases, it is the father who is absent (Kreider 2008).

It is overly concerning that, in most African American neighborhoods across the nation, most households are headed by single women who were probably raised by single mothers as well. Young

39

Black single mothers with one income often struggle to provide the same kind of lifestyle that two incomes will. Many young Black single mothers lack the educational qualifications to obtain a job that will pay them enough to provide a stable life for their children without receiving some form of government assistance. High quality daycare costs a lot of money and can be extremely difficult to pay for with only one income. This is a well-known fact and the primary reason that the Head Start program and Early Head Start were designed and implemented as a part of President Lyndon B. Johnson's war on poverty in 1965.

The Head Start program was intended to provide children from low-income families the emotional, social, health, nutritional, and psychological support they need. Head Start programs serve over a million children and their families each year in urban areas in all fifty states. What is even more concerning than all the Black single-parent households is the reality that the educational achievement gap persists fifty-five years later. The reality is that public education is failing inner-city Black children. The schools are not bad schools, and most of the teachers and administrators are competent and compassionate. The public school system is failing because of the attitudes and behaviors of parents and students.

For the longest time, I have been trying to understand why Black students do not perform on grade level despite all the money given to failing Black schools by the federal and state governments. Many inner-city youth seem to not be interested in using their brains when it comes to school curriculum. They have some sort of "lazy brain syndrome." It seems like they sit in class spaced out or are too busy talking while the teacher attempts to instruct them. They do not pay attention to the instructions and do not ask questions about what they do not know. They expect to slide by with mediocrity. The public school system is allowing this behavior to continue by promoting children who have not received passing grades. These African American students are on education welfare. They are not expected to learn anything. The ones who want to learn, do, but the ones who do not goof off and disrupt the learning of others. These nonlearners are so disruptive to the point the administration cannot effectively address their behavior issues.

Sadly, inner-city schools have become holding cells for future prisoners and impoverished adults. The same students who disrupt classes are the ones who will give their all in a sporting contest, however. What do we do with people who have the potential to work hard and be successful but choose not to educate themselves and follow the rules of school and the larger society? Black youth do well with physical education and physical instruction in the arts but not always in mental endeavors. It is not that they are not capable of critical thinking and higher learning, they just are not interested! We must stop holding Blacks to lower standards in the name of helping them. We are doing them no favors by passing them along in school, giving them grades that they did not earn and allowing them to go off to college unprepared. Affirmative action programs designed to help Black people, the poorest of Black people, have not been effective in doing so. They have only helped those Blacks who were already capable of doing well. Passing Black people along and allowing them to be held to lower standards does nothing but make them lazy, and it takes away their incentive to work hard to accomplish their goals.

Education has always been the number one tool used by those who want to better themselves in life. In 1865, when the slaves were free, all of them had the intense desire to learn and to obtain any form of education that they could. The whole race was trying to go to school, and because of that reason, historically, Black colleges and universities began to form and pop up all over the nation to educate the newly freed slaves. The ex-slaves knew that they had to educate themselves to help themselves progress in this newfound freedom. They were the first Southerners to campaign for universal public education. If it were not for the freed slaves, we would not have public school education like we do today in America.

The freedmen knew that educating themselves was the only way for them to make a way for themselves in American society. They were able to go out into the world and make a living for themselves. They were able to establish their own towns and organizations. They formed their own banks in certain areas, and they were able to sustain themselves within their own community.

Today, it seems as though our youth do not want education. It appears they look at education as something that White people want or something that only people need to have. I think they know that it is necessary to learn to function in society, but I think they equate being educated to being White. I think our youth today feel as though it is the ultimate evil to act White or do anything that would allow another Black person to think of you as acting White. Black children are afraid of being smart because they equate being smart to being lame and being educated to acting White. They would rather be cool than smart.

I tend to agree with people like Thomas Sowell who have long spoken about the ills of giving out handouts to poor Blacks. Giving handouts to poor Blacks only makes things worse for them. Instead of them taking the handouts and pulling themselves up, they tend to stay right where they are and want you to continue to give them things for free. It is like reaching down into a hole with your hand and trying to pull them up out of the hole, but instead of them grabbing your arm and trying to pull themselves out of the hole, they open their hand and ask for you to drop the goods down to them. It is like they just want to receive the goods. They want access to the same things that are available outside of the hole while staying in the hole.

Programs that are designed to help pull poor Black people out of the ghetto only seem to benefit Black people who are already able to pull themselves out of the ghetto. Those who have the intellectual ability and the drive to work hard and succeed will do so anyway without government assistance. Those who do not want to do well still will not do well even with government assistance.

I often wonder if Black politicians, Black superintendents, and Black administrators of majority Black schools see what is going on in Black schools and Black neighborhoods. Can they see that what they are doing is not working? I have concluded that they can see that it is not working. They know it is not working, but they feel like the system that is in place must stay in place, like there is no other way. They are not thinking outside the box. They think we cannot change the education system and the way it is set up, so we must just do small incremental things to try to change the system to meet the needs of the children instead of them thinking that you can change the children by changing the test they take. It does not work that way. The children do not care about the test. They do not even take the test seriously. Many Black children come to class and just want to be given the answers to the test. They prefer to be spoon-fed by their teachers rather than learn to use critical thinking skills and good study habits. They sleep or cut up in class, and when they fail their classes, they have the nerve to blame the teachers. When several students behave this way and fail, it is deemed the teacher's fault or the school's fault. The children are never blamed for their failure. Failing students create failing schools—bottom line. We must get the people in charge to understand the nature of the people they are trying to help. If you do not understand the nature of the problem, then you will never solve the problem.

African American students are not inferior to White students in any way. The only difference that I have seen is that White students learn because they want to learn. Black students do not learn because they do not want to learn. Black students who underperform seem to not understand why they need to be educated. Black students can learn and have access to more resources than they often realize. Black children who want to be educated and go off to college do so because of their individual determination. Just because a child is raised in a housing project does not mean their IQ is low. There are numerous examples of Black children who were raised in Bloomfield or grew up on the southside of Macon, Georgia, in Pendleton Homes, who graduated from high school and have gone on to college and graduated from college. It all comes down to the individual's mindset and their desire to get out of poverty and make something of themselves.

Children who come to school to eat breakfast and lunch and misbehave the rest of the time do not need an Individual Education Plan (IEP). What they need is to learn how to sit down and be disciplined. Schools cannot accommodate everybody's foolishness. You can only educate children who want to learn. The worst-behaved children can recite all the lyrics to a rap song on the radio, which means they can learn what they want to learn. It is time to stop propagating the idea that systemic racism is the cause of the persistent disparities between Black and White students. Individual behavior is the reason why people end up in the predicament they do. We cannot continue to blame White people for our failures. The White man is not the enemy anymore.

The truth is that Black children are failing because they are not being prepared for school by their parents and are being sent to school without understanding what school is for. We cannot ignore the fact that they come to school and act a fool. They will not sit and be quiet and allow the teacher to teach the children who want to learn. That is the real problem with Black schools. Behavior is the problem that must be addressed to transform Black schools and Black communities. The failure of Black students has got nothing to do with the teachers or the administrators. You can go all over this nation and look at majority Black schools, and they all have the same problems. Now why is that? Why is it that Macon, Georgia, has the same problems with their inner-city neighborhoods and schools as New York City? Two completely different parts of the country with the same cultural aspects and guess what? The children are failing.

This is sad, and nobody wants to admit the truth that statistics show. Neither school superintendents nor anyone in the political arena wants to address the truth and admit that some Black people are their own worst enemy. Black politicians get elected and feel the need to stand up for Black people at any cost, even when it means ignoring the facts about the role of Black people in their lack of progress. They are like the parent of the worst child in school who is always being called to the school about the child's misbehavior and yet always finds a way to blame any and everybody else but their child. They say, "Not my child. My child would not do anything like that." They make excuses for the child and, as a result, are teaching the child that his/her behavior is acceptable.

High dropout rates in majority Black schools lead to despair among African Americans when they cannot find gainful employment. Young Black males set themselves up for failure and then turn to the streets, either selling drugs or committing robberies, and end up in prison. Young women who drop out get pregnant early, and without any real means of providing for the child, they end up on welfare. Today, a college degree is what a high school diploma used to be. Having a degree does not guarantee you a good-paying job anymore, but not having one or postsecondary vocational training guarantees that you will live in poverty and only gain dead-end employment. If you are a male dropout and you spend a significant amount of your time with like-minded acquaintances on the corner, there is an excellent chance that you will have opportunities to participate in the illegal economy—the drug trade. Whether you participate or not, being in proximity to the drug business when the police come around is enough to put you in contact with the criminal justice system.

Family breakdown, lazy parenting, and failing schools are all factors that go into creating and perpetuating poverty in Black America. Poverty and the victim mindset that accompanies it partially explain why America's jails and prisons are full of Black men for whom incarceration is almost a rite of passage. Violent crime rages in impoverished Black neighborhoods seemingly to no end. Black-on-Black crime, not Black on White nor White cops on Black, is the most critical problem. Drug and gang culture in inner-city Black neighborhoods breed violence and a lack of respect for the law. It would be wrong to ignore the role that systematic racism played in creating the Black American ghettos, but it is also wrong to ignore the fact that a large majority of African Americans have made tremendous gains. Because of desegregation, the Black middle class is not only bigger and wealthier but also liberated from the separate but unequal nation that existed before the triumph of the Civil Rights Movement. The majority of African Americans are socially, economically, and culturally a part of the American mainstream and follow social norms like other Americans. Black culture or hip-hop culture that exists in American inner cities have become a counterculture that undermines Black success. So how are Black teenagers living in impoverished neighborhoods supposed to escape?

Our inner-city youth need a playbook that will give them instructions on how to escape poverty. They cannot follow the advice of parents who failed to escape and oftentimes do not have any consistent mentors in their lives who can teach them how to escape either. The teenager is likely being raised by a single mother, who herself was raised by a single mother. They cannot rely solely on their schoolteachers. They need constructive academic support at home, which, in many cases, they do not receive. The most important factor that must be considered is personal responsibility. Social programs only go so far in helping those living in poverty. Wrong choices and a lack of ambition are a major part of the reason why impoverished Blacks stay in poverty. Government policies will not improve the plight of poor Blacks until poor Blacks begin to take full advantage of the resources afforded to them and take responsibility for their lot in life. You cannot help people who do not want to be helped. One must follow the rules of society to become successful. We, as African Americans, must hold one another accountable for our choices and actions and stop making excuses for our fellow brothers and sisters when they fail to follow the rules.

CHAPTER 5

Community Reform

My childhood as a Black boy was unique because I was born into a middle-class Black family living in an all-White subdivision off Hartley Bridge Road in South Bibb County. In the mid-1980s, there were only a handful of Black families living in that area. I excelled in school and was always at or near the top of my class. I learned to speak proper English and to write grammatically correct sentences. I fit right in with the White students and formed friendships with most of them. After elementary school, my parents decided to send my sister and I to Byron Middle School, which is in neighboring Peach County, to avoid sending us to Ballard-Hudson Middle School, which is in a crime-ridden Macon neighborhood. Most of the White students from Porter entered private school for their middle and high school years. A small few of them attended Byron Middle School with me. Their parents opted to pay out-of-county tuition instead of private school tuition, the same as mine had. While attending school in Byron, I was one of two Black students in my class and one of only six Black students in my cluster. Most of the Black students were in clusters 8-2 and 8-3. Cluster 8-1 was for the more intelligent pupils or maybe I should say better-performing pupils. I enjoyed always having another Black student in class with me.

Toward the end of the eighth grade, I knew that I would be following my sister, who is eleven months older than me, to Central High School for my ninth-grade year. Central was, at that time, about 60 percent Black and 40 percent White and the best public high school in Macon. I knew that I would be in classes with many more Black students than I ever had before; therefore, I had to prepare myself. I would have to Blacken myself up a bit to fit in and not be ostracized for speaking proper English and dressing "White." Going into ninth grade, I changed my wardrobe, being sure to pick out clothes and shoes that the other Black kids wore such as FUBU, Nautica, Sean John, Karl Kani, Saucony shoes, and Jordan's. I learned to function as a Black male, walk and talk like a Black man, think like a Black man, listen to Black music, and pay more attention to Black girls and their curvaceous backsides. Beginning to like Black girls was significant because I became attracted to White girls first. To attract the Black girls, I felt the need to dumb myself down and give off the impression of being anti-intellectual while still making good grades because Mama and Daddy did not play that!

Why was it necessary for me to dumb myself down to fit in with inner-city Black kids and to attract more Black girls? Does inner-city Black culture impede Black educational achievement? Does welfare contribute to the lack of achievement by African American students? I think we all know that living in poverty causes students to not perform well in school. But is it just because they are in poverty? Does being on welfare have anything to do with a lack of drive or lack of willingness to except responsibility for oneself in the society? Being on welfare is the result of living in poverty, but I think that being on welfare leads people to continue to live in poverty. Coming from a low-income family is a strong predictor of educational performance. Children, whether they are Black or White, who live in poverty have an average lower educational achievement and are more likely to underachieve throughout school. Historically, Black schools were given less resources than White schools, and that helped create the Black-White achievement gap. After segregation ended and Black schools were closed and White schools were integrated, Black children who were given the same resources as White children began to improve, and the achievement gap began to close. It is now the year 2020, and the achievement gap still exists between Black students and White students at or near the same level it has for decades. Why is that?

In fact, the achievement gap has begun to widen and has been widening for some time now. Why is that? I believe that the achievement gap is not the consequence of a lack of resources in Black schools as it was in the past. For decades now, the government has created policies to fund inner-city Black schools known to have been underperforming schools filled with impoverished Black children with the money and other resources needed to level the playing field for those children. After giving those schools millions of dollars and loads of outside social support services for those children, they continue to fail. Therefore, I feel that the achievement gap is not caused by a lack of resources but rather by a lack of academic performance and a lack of drive to perform well in school.

The fact of the matter is many Black students in failing schools are underachievers. No amount of money given by the government can make students want to learn. Learning starts at home, and the will to learn is engrained in children by their parents. They learn to work hard by watching their parents. Children learn to do well by mimicking their parent's behavior. If their parents did well in school, the children are more likely to do well in school. If children grow up watching their parents work hard and showing them how to be responsible, they grow to do the same things. Those children who have responsible parents take school seriously and understand that self-responsibility is required to do well in school and in life.

African American students are most likely to receive a lower score on standardized tests and drop out of school at much higher rates than White counterparts. There is wide disagreement among scholars on the causes for persistent causes of the Black-White achievement gap. Many scholars and those in the education profession make excuses for students who come from poverty by stating that it is not their fault that they do not perform well in school rather it is the fault of a system that does not help those students in the same way it does more affluent students.

This is simply not true as we know, over the years, there have been many attempts to level the playing field between Black inner-city students and White students who do not live in poverty. As we look at Black schools across America, even Black students who come from middle-class families tend to perform lower than their White counterparts do. Focusing more on the homelife of the individual student certainly makes sense when trying to figure out why that student is failing for we know that individual motives are based upon individual desire and individual success is based upon the acceptance of one's own responsibility for themselves and their own success.

Many scholars choose to blame unequal access to resources as the reason for the persistent education achievement gap. They make claims such as every dollar spent on a Black student equals up to $7 spent on a White student. They continue to blame political history and current policies for the lack of funding or difference in funding between inner-city districts and more affluent or suburban districts. The No Child Left Behind Act was put in place to address that and has done as much as possibly could be done to address the lack of funding or the difference in funding between Black schools and White schools.

More recently, the Every Student Succeeds Act has done even more to fund inner-city schools and try to close this achievement gap. Yet the gap still exists, and Black students are continuing to fail at much higher rates than White students. I think it is fair to say that money is not the problem. With all the money that has been given to Black inner-city schools over the years and the fact that the achievement gap still exists says one thing to me. Children who do not value education do not do well in school. You can continue to throw money at these failings schools all you want, but until the children themselves want to do better in school, they will not. No teacher or administrator nor politician or amount of money can make a student do well in school.

Educating children starts at home with the parents. What parents do in front of the children and the way they make children feel about education have everything to do with their will to study and their performance in school. When you teach children from an early age that learning is a good thing and learning will help them do well in life, they tend to take education more seriously. When children grow up in environments that are not conducive to learning how to sit down and behave and listen to instructions and follow rules, they tend to perform poorly and misbehave in school and make bad decisions in life and find themselves living in poverty due to those bad decisions.

I do not think politicians and education officials want to change their thoughts about why lower-class African Americans are in the condition they are because they benefit from blaming racism. They say it's due to systemic racism and oppression. That is just an excuse. All of it is an excuse to blame White people because White people are easy to blame, and it is hard to tell the truth and say many impoverished African Americans are living in poverty because of their own behavior. Admitting that truth would, for one, tick off a lot of people who support increasing the budgets of social service programs, and it would also tick off the recipients of social services, but it is the truth. It is not hard to see the truth, but it is difficult to change. If we tell the truth about the ills of the Black community, who will want to continue taking taxpayer dollars and dumping it into poor Black neighborhoods knowing that the money is not doing any good? Negative behavior and poverty mindset are to blame for their continued impoverished condition.

If we shift the blame from an inherently racist system and place it upon the individual, policy makers and the social services field would be affected. Less money would be allocated to social services, and less social service jobs would be needed. Dumping money onto a problem in which money cannot solve can be compared to going to see a doctor for an illness where instead of the doctor treating the illness after running tests, he makes a guess as to what the illness is and prescribes a medicine for you to take. After a few weeks of no improvement, he makes another diagnosis and writes another prescription. A few more weeks go by with no improvement, and the doctor makes another guess and writes yet another prescription. Months go by with no improvement, yet you continue to trust this doctor and continue to pay for the prescriptions. How many wrong diagnoses must one endure before they change doctors? This is what, in my opinion, politicians are doing with Black poverty. They understand the causes of the problems but choose not to address them.

Racism is not preventing us from achieving anything. Racism in systems still exists but can be overcome. African Americans are resilient; we can overcome anything. Fighting racial discrimination will always be necessary, but I feel that organizations like the NAACP should evolve and create after-school tutoring and mentoring programs instead of continuing to complain about what White people do or do not do. The NAACP must evolve or die out. It is no mystery why the NAACP's branches are full of old Black folks who grew up in segregation. They are trying to hold on to the glory days of the Civil Rights Movement. For far too long, Black people have been brainwashed into believing that the White man is actively trying to disenfranchise and kill us. That kind of thinking gives White supremacists too much credit. Racism does exist, but it is not standing in our way. Black folks are so trained to think that the system will not work for them, many do not even attempt to make it work.

The truth is that African Americans do not exercise their right to vote in state and local elections, the ones that affect us the most, in the manner they should. It is true that neither political party tends to give enough attention to the socioeconomic issues facing Black America, but that simply means we must make both parties fight for our votes instead of allowing Democrats to take our votes for granted. Black folks seem to think that Republicans are all racist and, therefore, are our natural enemies. Who told them that? Why do they still believe this? An entire political party cannot be racist. If we take that to be true, then we must also address the fact that former President Lyndon Baines Johnson, the father of the modern welfare system in America, was a racist!

In my opinion, the Conservative parties can help African Americans more than Liberals. In the past couple of decades, Republicans have not needed the African American vote to win in rural America and the American South and, therefore, did not fight for it. However, I believe that will soon change, and they will begin to fight for our votes everywhere if they are smart. With growing numbers of minorities in this country, every political party is going to have to start appealing to African American and Hispanic voters if they want to win elections on the national level. This recent election of Joe Biden and Kamala Harris was a referendum against Donald Trump and was a clear indication that the Black vote matters in America. Without the Black vote, the Democrats would not have been able to defeat Trump.

For far too long, the Republican party has ignored the Black vote. The days of them being able to win national elections without a significant number of Black votes are gone. Any political party will need the Black vote going forward in future elections to win the presidency and the majority of house and senate seats. It is now time for every political party to begin to court, actively court, the Black population for our votes. If they do not do so, they will run the risk of losing many more elections to the Democrats who at least listen to Black voters and try to show that they support Black voters in their concerns. Black voters are not stupid and do realize that the Democrats do not always do everything that Black voters need them to do, but at least, we know that the Democrats attempt to not only listen to our concerns but will also provide social programs to try and implement the necessary changes that we seek.

It is my opinion that the Liberals mean well by implementing many social service programs, but those programs are not capable of providing any type of change that is necessary to uplift the inner-city Black communities. I feel that individual responsibility is the only way for Black America to become a thriving, successful community once again.

Black people fear and dislike Conservatives because they are thought of as being the same southern Conservatives from days past, you know, the ones who love the Confederate flag. Black people feel that the Conservative party of this nation is the new version of the segregationist Democrat party of the old South. It is no secret that southern Conservatives once voted primarily Democrat and fought to maintain segregation between Blacks and Whites.

If Republicans do nothing to counteract the bad reputation they have earned for being associated with racist segregationists and

White supremacists, they will forever miss out on opportunities to gain the Black vote and secure political power. They may continue to feel that the party does not need the Black vote, but they will soon realize that they do.

It is my opinion that future elections will rest upon the Black vote. It is time for Black voters to also stop thinking of our brothers and sisters who chose to vote for Republicans as Uncle Toms or traders to the race. It is okay to vote for other parties.

In my opinion, Conservative policies will do more for Black Americans than policies offered up by Liberals. Facts are facts, and it has been proven that policies enacted by Liberals have done nothing more than maintain the status quo and retard Black progress in the inner city. The Conservative package is quite inviting, and it looks like it is made specifically for us. We must take it upon ourselves to research what the Conservative parties stand for and give them our votes if they will respect us and cater to our needs. It is what it is at this point. We do not owe our allegiance to any one party; they must earn our vote. Conservative values of personal liberty, individual responsibility, economic liberty, and respect for the rights of other individuals and their property have always been and will always be for the foreseeable future necessary for success in this country.

We squander our political power and underestimate our economic power. It is time for the African American mindset to evolve. We have made outstanding political progress and socioeconomic progress, and now we must wake up from this "we can only vote for Democrats" slumber. We must dispose of the notion that because we are Black, we must vote for Democrats. Black people are not one homogeneous mass, all marching to the beat of the same drum. Our innate collectivism encourages us to do what is best for many of us, but we must also embrace individual responsibility. Individual responsibility is necessary to thrive in America. Collectively, we can build our neighborhoods and institutions up once we have built ourselves up individually. We are Black because of the melanin in our skin, not because we fit into some idea of what "being Black" should be. We are responsible for ourselves and our futures. I think we know by now that blaming systemic racism is played out. Blaming systemic racism for our failures is a cop-out excuse that ignores personal responsibility. Conservative principles are needed in the Black inner city to close the Black/White achievement gap and combat mass incarceration. It will never close if Black folks support the victimhood mindset being sold to us by Liberals. We must reform our thinking and use reason and logic to develop our communities.

CHAPTER 6

Behavior Issues in Black Failing Schools

Over the past forty-five years, student achievement in the United States has been tracked, and it shows that all students in every category have made notable gains in academic achievement, however, not all groups of students have made improvements at the same rate. Evidence of the racial achievement gap exists in standardized test scores, high school dropout rates, high school completion rates, college acceptance and retention rates, and disparities between income levels. The racial achievement gap exists as early as preschool. It is evident when children come to school for the first time whether someone has been working with them before they start school. Because education starts at home, a lack of teaching children how to read or to recognize words, numbers, and sounds at home before they even enter school leads to Black children having substantially lower test scores than their White counterparts.

In a study published in 2009, Reardon and Galindo specifically examine test scores by race and ethnicity. The data Reardon and Galindo (2009) use comes from the ECLS-K, sponsored by the National Center for Education Statistics. The ECLS-K has data collected from a sample of 21,400 students from the kindergarten class of 1998–1999. The students who participated in the research study had their reading and mathematics skills evaluated six separate times from 1998 to 2004. The study contains content areas based on the national assessment of educational progress in fourth grade content areas. The assessments were scored using a three-parameter item response theory model. Reardon and Galindo (2009) found that Black students begin kindergarten with math and reading scores lower than those of White students. When they tested the same students six years later, they found that the Black students were behind by about a third. African American children arrive at kindergarten and first grade with lower levels of oral language, reading, and mathematics skills than White and Asian American children.

Studies like this one claim that the achievement gap could be closed if the performance gap at school entrance is addressed. But what about Head Start programs? Isn't that what they are for? Head Start is a government-funded program that began in the late 1960s to do just that. Head Start was intended to begin educating inner-city children, mainly those who are Black and who come from low-income families to close the achievement gap between Black and White children when starting kindergarten. These programs are located throughout the nation and serve relatively the same population in every state. These programs are well-funded, yet the achievement gap at school entrance persists.

Many Black children do not do as well in school as White children because school is not thought about the same way for Black children as it for White children. In fact, Black people and White people are quite different. We think differently. We use different parts of our brain to determine how we see the world and how we fit into the world. European and some Asians tend to be more left minded or, better yet, are more inclined to use the left hemisphere of the brain more so than the right hemisphere, meaning they favor learning from outside of themselves, from someone else. They rely heavily on education. The Black race tends to use the right hemisphere of their brain more so than the left, meaning that they are more introverted or have an inner culture. The traditional African view of the world promotes harmony with the world around us. Black culture is shaped by the cultivation of the internal. There are three kinds of people in the world, one type tends to rely on the external sources of knowledge for their survival and success. The second kind tends to rely more on their omniscient intelligence, which is innate. The way we think shapes our cultures. Our culture influences our behavior, and our behavior determines our success. Africans and the Black race are more communal and tend to rely upon learning from within us for intuitive guidance. We see one another as our means of determining what is acceptable and what is not. Belonging to the group is more important than being an individual, whereas in White Western culture, being an individual is more important than belonging to the group.

Hemispheric differences of the brain are one of the main reasons for cultural differences among the races. There are many differences in the thought patterns between the White and Black races. For example, Black folks dress to be seen, making sure our outfits are matching from head to toe, what we call *clean*. White people do not seem to care much whether their shirt matches their shoes. We also love to put rims on our vehicles. A Black man will put twenty-four-inch rims that cost $2,000 and an $800 paint job on a 1984 Chevrolet Caprice that is only worth $1,000 all in the name of being flashy. White men are content to ride around town on factory wheels and do not seem to know what candy paint is.

We need a different form of education for Black kids. Black people predominantly do not use the same side of the brain that White people predominantly do. Black people are predominantly right-brain thinkers, and White people are predominately left-brain thinkers. The left and the right hemispheres of the brain differ from each other in that one is intellectual and the other is sensuous. The left is realistic, and the right is impulsive. The left is deductive, whereas the right is imaginative. The left is rational, whereas the right is intuitive. Not all Black people are right-brain thinkers just as not all White people are left-brain thinkers. However, White people are predominantly left-brain thinkers, and Black people are predominantly right-brain thinkers.

Education for Black children must cater to their right-brain thinking. Black students are being educated in a society that is predominantly left sided, which explains why they do not fare as well as White students do in American schools. School systems must begin to include methods that make more use of the right hemisphere of the brain. It has been recently discovered that educational methods that appeal to the right side of the brain trump those of the left. These methods have been recently discovered in Western society; however, these techniques have been used in Africa since time immemorial. School systems that serve predominantly Black children should look to Africa to find out what method they used to teach the African and implement those methods in teaching the African American. We must realize now and forevermore that there is a cultural unity among all White nations and all Black nations and all Oriental nations. There exist common factors that are traceable to the hemisphere of the brain that dominates the thinking, cultural expressions, and languages of each of the above nations. The behavior of the Black nation is a product of our biological make up, which creates our cultural expressions and the way we react to others.

I am not an education specialist, and these are just my thoughts and opinions. I think everyone involved in education is at a loss for ideas on how to improve the educational system for Black children. My experience comes mainly from working as a site coordinator for both communities in schools of Central Georgia and communities in schools of Atlanta and operating a nonprofit after-school program (Supporting Our Youth, Inc.), serving inner-city youth.

In our after-school setting, we experience many of the same problems that teachers do in the school setting. I am convinced that Black children learn differently and need a different environment than most public schools are currently providing to reach their maximum potential. In Black schools, you should have a smaller class size because the kids cannot focus when there are distractions going on within the classroom. You cannot have many Black kids in one class and expect for them to learn. For you to be able to make them learn, you must first make them behave. For you to be able to make them behave, you always need two teachers in the classroom. Maybe

59

that needs to be implemented for Black schools that are failing. Class size should be reduced for those schools purposely for the good of the students or hire more paraprofessionals to assist with classroom management. I believe that will probably work the best. You must have at least two adults in the room for Black students to stay on task.

When I worked as an AVID program tutor at Rutland High School, that is how we managed to keep the students engaged and on task throughout the class period. We had some rough kids, but because there was always more than one adult in the room, it made a huge difference in keeping everybody on task because you always had an adult walking around the room, asking "what are you doing," peeping over their shoulders, making sure the students were doing their assignments. They had no other choice. Every time they turned around, another adult was on top of them ready to correct their behavior. That is what it takes for Black kids because they tend to misbehave more frequently than White and Asian students. You must be on them like drill sergeants (tough-love drill sergeants) all the time, constantly correcting their behavior.

Behavior will have to be addressed because you cannot teach Black kids with the way they behave in school now. You cannot teach these Black children anything without first creating a highly structured and disciplined environment. I hate to say it, but Black children who come from unstructured households must be disciplined in a stern way. You must treat Black children who come from low-income areas like they are in the military. It is sad to say, but schools will have to use discipline standards like boot camp to get the worst of the worst students to respond to structure because they do not have structure at home. They are not being taught structure as small children. From the very beginning, parents must provide structure and discipline. That is why the parents are dysfunctional themselves. They neither have discipline nor can create an environment at home that teaches the child how to embrace structure and learn self-discipline. Therefore, they come to school and are expected to know how to fit into a structured environment without knowing what structure is.

African children live in greater poverty, yet they go to school and find a way to be successful. They learn and then come to America and become doctors. The fact that Black people in America can attend school free of charge should be incentive enough to make our children want to be educated; it is not though. Even Black people admit that Black children behave terribly in school. Saying it is due to racism is making them not perform well. It is giving them a cop-out excuse to fail. It is White people and educated Black people who are at the top of education organizations saying that poverty is the problem, and nobody wants to address the actual issue: children in Africa who live in neighborhoods and towns that have all dirt roads in the villages and dirt floors in their homes. Whatever the case, those African children are going to school, and they are serious about school because they know that it is going to lead them to having more.

It is my belief that many leaders in education and politics are out of touch with the realities that exist in the American ghetto. Lobbyist and politicians who do not understand the ghetto and are not observing the ghetto daily think that because Black children come from the inner city and they live below the poverty line, giving them extra resources will magically save them from the ghetto and social ills that run rampant. Extra resources are great for those who are of the mindset and who are in position to take full advantage of those resources. Resources alone cannot save poor Black people. They must have the individual desire to save themselves.

Historically, African Americans have been discriminated against, but now that is no longer the case. When it comes to a Black person's ability to make something of themselves, the only difference between pre-civil rights era and post-civil rights era is the absence of the oppressive laws. Even before integration, Black people were able to make something of themselves. Their career options were limited in many ways, but that did not stop them from taking education seriously and finishing whatever level of schooling they could. Our ancestors really wanted to learn, and they were able to find ways to learn despite oppression and racism throughout America.

61

We have our own colleges and universities where we can go and earn degrees and become something. We can become a doctor if we want to. We can become lawyers and any other type of professional with degrees earned at our illustrious historically Black colleges and universities. There may not have been a lot of positions for us in the White world during the Jim Crow era, but now we can go out and find work wherever we desire and do whatever we desire if it is not breaking any law. We did it after being treated like animals, being denied the opportunity to learn how to read and write. Under oppression, we still did it, but now the Black kids are going to schools led by Black principals and being instructed by Black teachers and living in a society that does not tell you that you must step off the sidewalk when a White person is walking toward you. You do not have to use a different entrance. You do not have to drink out of a different water fountain than White people. The police do not lock you up just because you looked at them the wrong way or simply because a White person accused you of committing a crime; well that is still happening today. White women, given the satirical name, Karen, have made a resurgence as of late in their attempts to get Black people in trouble with the law as it suits them. Normally, however, police officers do not threaten to smash your head in because you, as a Black man, do not refer to them as "sir."

We do not live in a society like that anymore, yet Black children come to school and act like they are living in a society that is oppressing them. They look at White people as being different. They recognize that White people think differently and behave differently from Black people. Black children who cut up in school will behave when a White administrator walks in the classroom because they expect for the White person to look at them as being different, and they know they are expected to follow the rules in the presence of White people. Black students think that Black teachers should understand their behavior, whether it is wrong or right, and hold them to different standards because the teachers are Black. The students feel that Black teachers should know that they are going to cut up and should be okay with them being who they naturally are because they are also Black. Black students feel that it is acceptable for them to misbehave around Black teachers and expect the Black teacher to just ignore it because that is the way we behave as Black people. They expect you to sit there and have no bad feelings about them because they misbehave. They do not respect the Black authority figure unless he or she is a true disciplinarian or is constantly appeasing them.

I believe Black children do not respect Black authority because we, as African people, are communal. As a communal people, we have the mindset of "you are no better than I am" and "you do not matter anymore than I do." Your position in life is the same as mine, and we look at White people as being the authority figures. When we, as African Americans, think about authority, we naturally envision White people being in charge. That vision of authority explains why little Black kids get quiet when a White person walks into the room because they assume, "Oh, that's somebody important. We need to be quiet and act like we have sense." If you are a Black teacher, Black students may respect you, but at the same time, they expect leniency from you when addressing their behavior and academic performance.

What if the United States stopped funding public schools? What if every school in America charged tuition to attend? If Black people had to pay to attend school, would that make a difference in the Black-White achievement gap? I believe that if Black parents had to pay for their children to go to school, the students would perform better in school. Maybe that is what it will take for them to take educational achievement more seriously. What if public schools provided real discipline where the disrespectful kids were sent home, and their parents were told their child cannot come back for a long time if you get to come back at all. What if public school administrators did not have to be afraid of ghetto parents and their ugly behavior? If school administrators had the ability to expel students who habitually demonstrate disruptive behavior, they could control the learning environment for Black children enough to make them learn. You must force them because the African brain thinks creatively, so you must make it think critically, whereas the White brain thinks critically, so you must teach it creativity.

Some Black people are just impractical when it comes to education. They want to have fun in everything they do. Everything about our culture is fun. We are jovial, sociable, and vivacious people. We like to laugh, crack jokes, dance, and party. We just want to know where the party is, whereas White people want to come in and take over everything, make plans, and go above and beyond to make a name for themselves. White people want to gain power and influence and oversee things. Black people do not want to be in control of everything; we just want to enjoy life and be comfortable. We go to work only because we must. We do our jobs at work, but we do not work ourselves too hard. We do what is required, enough not to get fired.

Maybe we should do away with truancy laws and stop making it illegal for parents to not send their children to school. Maybe we, as a nation, should stop forcing people who do not respect education to attend school. What if we reduce food stamps and other government benefits drastically and reallocate those funds to help pay for the tuition for school? I believe everyone would take school more seriously if they were paying for it. Low-income parents could receive a stipend by working a qualifying number of hours each month to supplement the tuition for school. If tuition were made mandatory for all schools in America, then maybe that would help close the achievement gap between Black and White students.

In Bibb County, Georgia, most White students attend private school, and their parents are paying for their tuition. I am sure those parents ensure their children are taking full advantage of the educational opportunities being afforded them. Maybe Black inner-city parents should be required to buy into the education system. Maybe they should just do away with the Title I funding all together because, at this point, the federal and state governments have given failing schools the resources they need to succeed, but the students are still not closing the achievement gap. The only things that I see that Black students are lacking are discipline and motivation. They have computers, brand-new, state-of-the-art buildings (in some places), and all the additional resources, yet the educational achievement gap has not closed. It has widened. The situation has gotten worse and continues to baffle many in the education field. With all the additional funds being sent to majority Black failing schools with Black administrators and Black teachers, it is not making much difference.

CHAPTER 7

Addressing Behavior Issues in Black Failing Schools

Black nationalism advocates a racial definition or redefinition of national identity. There are different indigenous nationalist philosophies, but the principles of all Black nationalist ideologies are unity and self-determination. Race pride for African Americans and Black power was a reaction against White racial prejudice and was critical of the gap between American democratic ideals and the reality of segregation and discrimination in America. The historical roots of Black nationalism can be traced back to nineteenth-century African American leaders such as abolitionist Martin Delany, who advocated the emigration of northern free Blacks to Africa, where they would settle and assist native Africans in nation-building. Delany believed that this development would also uplift the status and condition of African Americans who remained, calling them "a nation within a nation...really a broken people" (Painter, Martin R. Delany).

Twentieth-century Black nationalism was greatly influenced by Marcus Garvey, a Jamaican immigrant to the United States who founded the United Negro Improvement Association (UNIA) in 1914. In an essay titled "The Future as I See It," Garvey insisted that the UNIA was "organized for the absolute purpose of bettering our condition, industrially, commercially, socially, religiously and politically." Garvey and the UNIA promoted the establishment of Black-owned businesses and Pan-Africanism. He had a vision of Black pride and economic independence for all Black people. Black nationalist organizations like the Nation of Islam and the Black Panther Party promoted racial self-respect and increased power for Blacks in economic and political realms. Matin Luther King, Jr. was successful at achieving civil rights legislation because of the ever present and strengthening threat of war, a race war between White supremacists and Black revolutionaries, such as the NOI and the Black Panthers. Today, I think that Black nationalist ideals and Afrocentric education can be utilized to address behavioral issues in Black failing schools and the cultural impetus driving them.

Black children lack the educational motivation needed to be successful in school. Veronica Knapper studied in her dissertation, *Factors That Influence Student Academic Motivation and How Those Factors Impact the Student Achievement of Third Grade Students (2017)*, teaching strategies that are used to motivate students, as well as the behaviors of motivated students. This study identified two factors that influence student academic motivation: parent involvement and home environment. Understanding the factors that contribute to student success and failure is of the utmost importance because this information can help educators, parents, and community organizations develop effective strategies that will improve student and, more specifically, Black student achievement. The qualitative research results of this study indicate that educators and schools should focus on increasing parental involvement and creating a school environment where students feel safe and can be motivated. We are living in an era where schools are held to accountability processes designed to improve student achievement and graduation rates. Veronica Knapper's study provides insight on how schools should engage in this endeavor by pointing out that student achievement starts at home. Parents are a child's first teachers, and their level of involvement has a great impact on student achievement and motivation (Knapper 2017).

Another dissertation, *The Majority to Minority Transfer: A Comparison in Black Achievement in Majority White and Majority Black High Schools* (1986), gives a historical account of the Black achievement gap as it addresses the question of Black achievement in integrated schools. It cites the *Equality of Educational Opportunity Report* from 1972, which states that minority group students do better in schools where they are not the majority. That same report goes on to point out that family background, social class, and student attitudes were the major determinants of educational achievement. Many desegregation programs were based upon the findings of this report, such as mandated busing and the majority to minority transfer program. During integration, Black high schools began to lose their high achieving students to majority White schools, which resulted in inferior test performance. It can be concluded from this dissertation that Black achievement in majority Black schools is linked to the socioeconomic factors of the students and not necessarily the quality of education provided at majority Black schools. It is often perceived that majority White schools have more qualified teachers, better curriculum, and a more disciplined environment than majority Black schools; however, this dissertation concludes that majority Black high schools have teachers who are just as qualified as those at majority White schools, offer a varied curriculum that prepares the students for college, and, as an added benefit, Black teachers in Black schools are more caring toward Black student's achievement (Turman 1986).

My take from this is that Black students can learn when held to the same standards as White children. Black children need the same structure and discipline that White children receive to achieve academic success. The US Department of Education, individual state departments of education, and local school boards have removed all barriers to educational achievement once faced by Black students during segregation.

Today, the only difference between majority White schools and majority Black schools is the lack of discipline and lack of motivation among Black students in majority Black schools caused by a poverty mentality. Black children in majority Black schools do not seem to understand the importance of education. They act as if education is just something being forced upon them, something that they neither need nor want. I believe that Black students who come from middle class and upper middle-class families and neighborhoods that attend majority Black schools do not perform much better than Black students from poor inner-city communities because of peer pressure to be "Black" and "cool." Their idea of what it means to be "Black" is detrimental to Black success in America.

This point can be proven by observing Black students from middle-class neighborhoods who attend majority Black schools. They often become intimidated by the culture and "standards" of inner-city Black students. The bad study habits and disdain for academics rub off on the seemingly high-achieving middle class rather than the love for academic achievement and the desire to learn rubbing off on the low-achieving, poor, inner-city kids. In other words, good does not rub off on bad; bad rubs off on good. That is what makes majority Black schools less successful than majority White schools. Now that we know what the problem is, we need to begin to formulate and implement Afrocentric solutions that will improve majority Black schools, solutions that will enable Black students to be smart and cool at the same time.

CHAPTER 8

Afrocentric Education

Racism leads to deep-seated self-hatred. "The Hate U Give" (White racism and violence), a concept espoused by Tupac Shakur, has given rise to a self-hatred that created the mentality that is responsible for the crime we are experiencing across America today. Younger African Americans are responding to past transgressions of racist White people. Those transgressions created the cesspool that is called the *ghetto*. White hatred created the ghetto to segregate and relegate African Americans to a second-class existence. People who are desperate and see no hope do not care about mainstream values. People who are oppressed by legitimized violence against them do not feel the need to assimilate into the dominant culture that oppresses them. Gang and drug culture in Black inner-city communities are the response of angry, oppressed people who feel that the American dream is not meant for them.

The Hate U Give is responsible for the failing schools in every major city in America. The Hate U Give denied African Americans true citizenship. The Hate U Give stifled dreams. The Hate U Give prevented healthy self-development and forced African Americans to become instruments of their own oppression. The Hate U Give created the THUG life mentality that is responsible for the high crime rates we are experiencing around America.

69

Just to be clear, White racism is to blame for the ills of the inner city, but we, as African Americans, have the responsibility to love one another, and it is our collective responsibility to take care of one another by rebuilding our neighborhoods that were destroyed purposely by the drug trade and, subsequently, the War on Drugs. Deindustrialization and globalization created high unemployment rates among African Americans in America's cities. Unemployment, redlining, and The Hate U Give created the unstable environments that are the American ghetto.

The Hate U Give created desperation that fuels the illegal drug trade and the American genocide. The killing of Black men by other Black men is equivalent to genocide. According to the Centers for Disease Control and Prevention, the firearm homicide rate for African American males aged ten to twenty-four years are 20.6 times as high as the rate among White males of the same age in 2019, and this ratio increased to 21.6 in 2020 (CDC 2022). The unprecedented rate of imprisonment of African American males further cripples the Black family from remaining intact and having the ability to maintain stability. People will behave in antisocial ways if you don't allow them to behave in social ways. Crime is the product of no work and dysfunctional schools. American society created the ghetto; therefore, America must rectify the problem by properly educating and incentivizing African American students to take full advantage of what America has to offer.

It is time for us, as Black people, to stop seeing ourselves as a people who are oppressed in America. We have a rich history that began in Africa. Granted, we may not know exactly what country in Africa or what region of West Africa we come from specifically, but we do know that we originated in parts of West Africa. We have an extraordinarily rich history, which our ancestors were a part of. No other racial group in America identifies themselves by their struggles alone; they identify themselves by their cultural backgrounds, experiences, and achievements. Why do we not do the same? It is true that our ancestral culture was stolen from us 402 years ago when our ancestors were captured and brought to this land as slaves, but because of modern technology, we can now research our ancestors using DNA and find out exactly what part of Africa, mainly West Africa, we come from, and we can find ways to reconnect to our people living there today. Our existence today does not have to be defined by the horrors and the trauma of our past. Doing so creates a negative attitude toward not only ourselves but also toward America and mainstream American society.

Dr. Charles Finch, a former professor at the Morehouse School of Medicine, once said, "Blacks must re-construct their historic memory. No nation, no race can face the future unless it knows what it is capable of. This is the function of history." Without knowledge of who we are and where we come from, we are lost. For this very reason, Black children in America need Afrocentric education that will raise Black consciousness and self-esteem. When Black children are taught that they are beautiful and made to feel that they can be proud of themselves and proud of their Blackness, they will feel good about themselves and their Blackness and, therefore, will do better in school and in life.

Afrocentric education needs to be introduced in the inner-city schools because the current curriculum is not relevant to our Black children. They are not interested in education because they do not see how it connects to them and their culture. They are bored, and to engage them, we need to show them how education connects them to the rest of the world and make it plain to them how our situation as Africans in America keeps us from being as productive as we could be due to still having to overcome the many barriers that were placed before us by past oppression. It is my opinion that we should implement African studies courses and select courses from critical race theory in our inner-city schools to teach our Black children about how racism in America shaped the Black community and, therefore, placed a lot of them in a disadvantaged situation.

Part of this Afrocentric education should also include courses in economics that teach Black youth about entrepreneurship and trade with Africa. I believe that it is time for us, as Africans in America, to embrace our African heritage and connect with our motherland so that we can take advantage of the resources and the power and beauty and wealth that can be obtained from doing business among ourselves. Trade with Africa can be beneficial to both our people on the African continent and those of us in the diaspora. This trade would produce jobs for our brothers and sisters in Africa and enable us here in America to produce our own products and sell them around the world with the production occurring in Africa. It's time that we connect to Africa in every way. That means spiritually through reconnecting to our west African religions that we practiced when we came here and embracing the history of our respective homelands. As the saying goes, "A man with no past has no present, and a man with no present has no future." Without knowledge of our past and any connection with our ancestors and without a love and understanding of the place from which we come, we can have no future in this world.

There is an entire continent filled with beautiful Black people doing beautiful Black things, an entire continent filled with Black nations, governed by Black people, and with industries run by Black people. We have real-world examples of Black societies functioning at every level equal to that of European society. As African Americans, we have an untapped resource, Africa. Africa can be a source of trade for our Black-owned businesses here in America and vice versa. We cannot go on another day being disconnected from our motherland. We need her, and she needs us.

Educating our children about Africa and the abilities of the Africans will change their perception of our plight here in America as well as our plight globally. We need Afrocentric education in Black schools, and we need it now. If our children do not know the hopes and dreams of our ancestors, then how can they fulfill them? Teaching our children about their ancestors and the culture from which they came will build their self-esteem and do more for our future as Black Americans than any march or protest could ever do. We must teach our children to build a future that is connected to Africa. We must connect our resources here in America to our African family and combine their resources with ours to grow all our communities. Our future begins with learning about our past. We can only help ourselves when we learn about ourselves. When we know who we are, we will recognize what we are capable of.

Our existence as Africans in America is a double-edged sword! One end represents White hatred and discrimination toward us, and the other end represents our self-hatred and disrespect for ourselves. We must cover one end to be able to use the sword to our benefit. We must cover our end. We cannot control the way White people behave toward us or how they feel about us, but we can control how we behave toward one another and how we feel about ourselves! Self-love and a return to our traditional African values and spirituality are the first steps toward covering our end of the sword.

Some common minority group responses to prejudice are avoidance, deviance, defiance, and self-hate. Some choose deviance because of experiencing discrimination from the dominant society. Others choose acceptance and allow prejudice and discrimination to continue because they feel powerless. I think the most common minority-group response to prejudice and discrimination among African Americans is angry protest (defiance), which, more times than not, accomplishes little more than drawing attention to the frustrations of the inner-city community. We protest, burn, and loot businesses in our neighborhoods or sit inside the church and pray, none of which brings about the necessary change we want to see. We complain and have a huge pity-party for about two or three weeks, and then we turn the other cheek and wait for the next injustice to occur.

In my opinion, our response should be to work within our own communities to utilize the resources and money that we have to help ourselves become less dependent on White America instead of try-ing force them to empathize with us, let alone solve our problems. Protesting, marching, and rioting are outdated strategies for making progress for the Black community. We must realize that economic segregation and economic disparity lead to substandard education, substandard health care, and substandard treatment by law enforce-ment officers (i.e., police brutality)! Instead of complaining, march-ing, and protesting, we should be buying properties, opening and supporting Black-owned businesses, and opening charter schools to provide better education for our youth!

Recently, I had the opportunity to attend a social and emotional learning summit, which addressed the need for social and emotional learning within schools. The conversation centered around building deeper connections with children and families who are served by school districts. Making the students feel heard, listening to them, and asking them what they care about was the focal point of the conversation. There were several speakers who addressed different areas of social and emotional learning. What I found to be most enlightening was a perspective that parents often have an inflated view of their child's school performance and are not aware that their students are below grade level. This made me realize that a lot of the pushback that social workers, counselors, teachers, and other professionals inside the schools often receive comes from a place of ignorance about the academic achievement or lack thereof by students.

Another perspective that I had not thought of is that parents who have not completed higher education often feel oppressed by the school system and school personnel when they are confronted with their child's lack of achievement and bad behavior. Parents who themselves did not have a great educational experience or who might have dropped out of school don't always feel like they are working together with teachers and principals to educate their children. These parents may feel a sense of anxiety about school themselves and, therefore, may avoid contact with the school subconsciously due to their past experiences. This could possibly explain the lack of parental engagement in schools.

Some takeaways from the summit were how to conduct empathy interviews, finding ways to make parents feel heard by the schools, and allowing families to serve as equal partners in leading educational change. I believe that, as school social workers and education policy advocates, we should lead the charge of bringing about educational change that will allow us to close the educational achievement gap between White, Black, and Brown students. We do this by creating culturally relevant curriculum and equity-focused policy. Afrocentric education that includes the community school strategy and programs such as communities in schools will help build strong relationships between the schools and the communities they are located in. Bringing the community in to support the school's mission of educating the next generation is vital for their success. As the African proverb states, "It takes a village to raise a child."

Afrocentric education is a critical foundation of learning that, I believe, will cultivate a strong cultural identity for students by immersing them in African traditions, rituals, values, and symbols. We, as a nation, must provide better learning outcomes for individuals, which will result in a stronger community for us all. According to the 2018 Sankofa Emerging Leader awardee Mr. Marshall Shorts, "Afrocentric Education is defined as the adoption of Afrocentric ideology and cultural relevancy for use within classrooms." It is my belief that Afrocentric education should be incorporated into school curriculum for public schools serving majority African American students. To effectively educate African American children, educators must provide a more authentic and relevant education for the children.

The problems faced by urban school districts that are tasked with educating a majority African American population are not caused by the children not having the resources necessary to learn. The problem is how they're being taught and what they're being taught. The curriculum used in the public school system is not relevant to many urban African American students; it is neither interesting to them nor does it teach them how to lift themselves from their current socioeconomic status. The current curriculum does not empower urban African American students to feel that they are important or encourage them to see themselves as an integral part of mainstream America. It does not educate them about themselves. It is not encouraging them to live as a people with a strong history, a people with a long successful history. Public school education, in its current form, does not empower many African American students to reach their full potential because educating African Americans from a European perspective reinforces their history of being second-class citizens in America, and it makes them feel as though Africans are second-class human beings in the world, always second to White people. This is what we must change. The purpose of Afrocentric education is to give African American students a mission through education that will give them the opportunity to lead themselves and not to feel the need to be second class to anyone in the world.

If African American students continue being miseducated, they will be excluded from good-paying jobs and being able to obtain generational wealth in the future. Education in America is used to control access to jobs and to create wealth. Without a solid education, many urban African American students will miss out on wealth-generating opportunities and will not be able to effectively compete for high-paying careers.

CHAPTER 9

Education Reform

In the study *Teacher Education Reform in Urban Educator Preparation Programs*, Tachell Banks sets out to discuss the importance of educator preparation programs devoting attention to reforming preparation programs to include high-need urban school clinical experiences for practicing teacher candidates. The focus of this study is to better prepare teaching candidates to meet the needs of students in high-need schools. The author has the opinion that public policy makers and the education community should take collective ownership for recruiting, preparing, and supporting new professional practitioners by providing them with better training on how to teach in an urban environment.

In this study, university- and college-based teacher preparation programs are being examined due to their failure to adequately prepare new teachers for the demands of modern schools. The author of this study states that there is evidence to show that teacher quality is one of the biggest in-school determinants of student achievement. She believes that colleges throughout the nation have inadequate preparation for their teaching candidates. She lists reasons why these programs are not doing a good job of preparing our nation's teachers. Her first reason is that these programs were designed around "disconnected curricula, a lack of socialization of teachers and pre-service

77

training, separation of theory and practice, and policy controlling decisions rather than what we know about teaching and learning" (Darling-Hammond 2005; Goodlad 1991).

Banks gives additional evidence as to why she feels teacher preparation programs are not doing an adequate job of preparing teachers for the reality of teaching in urban school districts. She states that traditional teacher preparation programs focus on subject matter and teaching methods but provide few connections to course content, and teacher candidate field placements are not well designed to foster skill development. This presents a gap between research and practice that leaves teacher candidates feeling unprepared for the classroom, especially classrooms filled with students with high needs. This study goes on to explain that teacher candidates need multiple and diverse classroom experiences coupled with their pedagogical coursework to better prepare them on how to manage classrooms and provide high-quality instruction in any school environment. Mentors and supervising teachers should be utilized in a well-crafted way to ensure that new candidates receive the support they need to become content experts and effective practitioners.

The purpose is to measure a teacher preparation program by utilizing quantitative survey results from candidates who were asked to rate their urban field experience. The candidates in this study were part of a program developed to increase teacher candidates' willingness to teach in urban schools. The study used seventy-three undergraduate and graduate teacher-education-program students for what they called Summer in the City (SITC). This was a paid field experience in a high-need urban school district that partnered with the local college. The purpose of the program was to provide these candidates with real-world urban classroom experience to persuade them to work in this type of setting due to the lack of well-qualified teachers in urban schools. Students were given a presurvey and post-survey, and the quantitative survey results show that candidates who attended urban schools during their P through 12 years were more willing to teach urban students as compared to candidates who did not attend urban schools. The program's success was measured by the quantitative survey results of the candidates. The survey showed that there was no significant change in candidates' willingness to teach in urban schools after completion of SITC.

An explanatory theory was used to examine the way that racial, cultural, and class identities shape the perspectives of teacher candidates and to critique those sources of economic and racial inequities within schools and communities to understand how these factors affect student learning in urban schools. This study used teacher candidates who were prepared to teach, and due to teacher shortages in urban school districts, it is likely that some, if not many of them, will find positions in urban areas. For new teachers to be more effective in urban school districts, they need to have a desire to be there, first and foremost, and be better prepared to manage behavior in the classroom. Classroom management is critical in urban school districts with high discipline rates. In my opinion, misbehavior by students and the lack of classroom management skills of teachers are two important reasons behind urban students' lack of academic achievement.

Education reform must begin with neighborhood reform. To transform urban schools and improve student outcomes, environments that are conducive to learning must be created first. Students cannot learn in chaotic classrooms. Teachers cannot teach in chaotic classrooms. In my experience, school administrators do a good job of creating a safe environment for students, but they cannot always control the behavior and the mentality that is being learned in the surrounding community and brought into the school building.

It's time for community stakeholders to get more involved in their neighborhood schools. The schools do not belong to the superintendent or the school principals. Yes, the school principals oversee the schools, but the schools do not belong to them. The schools belong to the community, and the community should have more say about what is happening in the schools. The community has a vested interest in its schools because the school is the training ground for the next generation who will become our leaders soon. We must begin to surround our schools with a community of support to empower students to succeed in school and in life. It is up to us to work together as individuals and organizations to bring in the necessary resources to illuminate and eliminate all barriers that prevent our students from receiving the best possible education and being well prepared for college and whatever career they choose. We are currently in a state of crisis, and our next generation stands to become a largely miseducated and an undereducated burden to society. We must act now to save our children and our communities, to prevent miseducation from taking away the opportunity for our children to have a strong and prosperous future.

We will not make any real reform to education in urban environments until we begin to rebuild inner-city areas that have been economically depressed for decades. The only way to ensure that students in urban school districts receive the best possible education is to ensure that they have a stable environment that is conducive to learning not only at school but also at home. Unsafe home environments and unsafe neighborhoods impact students negatively by exposing them to all types of traumas that their developing brains are not equipped to deal with.

Jean Anyon, a former professor in the doctoral program in urban education at the Graduate Center of the City University of New York and civil rights and social activist, undressed this issue in her book *Ghetto Schooling: A Political Economy of Urban Educational Reform*. In this book, Jane speaks about the need to redress the effects of destructive ghettoization of cities and their poorer residents. Her theory involves eliminating political and economic isolation that produces ghettoization. Jean's vision of educational reform is based on the idea of increasing low socioeconomic children's social and economic well-being and status while they are students and before they become adults. The elimination of poverty and the negative psychological effects of poverty are key to eliminating underperforming schools. Of course, it might just be wishful thinking to believe that we could eliminate poverty in all urban areas.

While this is true that something must be done, I believe it is the job of the community stakeholders to bring about fundamental social change in the community they call home. I believe that the stakeholders must work hand in hand with school officials and community organizations that aim to increase student outcomes in urban school districts. School superintendents and district personnel must begin listening to what community members have to say and allowing community stakeholders to have the opportunity to serve as liaisons and be given the opportunity to take an active role in improving the neighborhood schools with a community-school focus. Without community members being involved and being allowed to present their knowledge, firsthand knowledge of the surrounding area and what they know needs to be improved, new teaching strategies and limited support services within the school will not create the long-term change that is needed. Without a long-range strategy that involves community partnerships with the schools, urban school districts will continue to miseducate urban African American students who will ultimately perpetuate the cycle of poverty (Anyon 1997).

Anyone goes on to say that a concerted national effort is needed to revitalize America's urban economies that will allow inner-city residents to share in prosperity. I share her thinking in that without improving the surrounding neighborhood, students are still feeling the same level of disdain for education no matter what improvements you make to their school building or what support services you bring into the school building. If students continue to live in squalor, they will continue to have a poverty mindset that prevents them from feeling as though what they are learning in school will help them improve their lives.

Real education reform will come about when school districts begin to work with community organizations made up of parents, retired teachers, retired school principals, and other community stakeholders such as business owners to create strategies that will not only improve the school setting but also bring about lasting social change for the entire community. After all, it takes a village to raise a child, and it is time to bring the village back into the equation. More community development organizations are needed to begin working together to shed light on what parents and students and other community stakeholders feel about the state of education today. These organizations can be the voice of the people and can use their numbers and potential influence to bring about necessary change by addressing the issues at local school board meetings. There is power in numbers, and the people hold the power. We must remember that the public school system serves the public. It belongs to the public, and it answers to the public. If the public is not happy with what the school district is doing, it is the public's right to voice their dissent and to force change to be made.

CHAPTER 10

Where Do We Go from Here—Communities Serving Schools Act

In April of 2022, Representative Susie Lee (D-NV) and Representative Tony Gonzalez (R-TX) reintroduced the Communities Serving Schools Act with bipartisan support. The Community Serving Schools Act is a bill that would potentially authorize $1 billion in grants that would be issued by the secretary of education for four-year periods to eligible state or local educational agencies to provide "wraparound services that address out-of-school factors that interfere with learning." This bill could serve as an avenue for educational agencies, such as Communities in Schools, to receive funding that would allow 25 percent of all Title I schools with $100,000 each for a site coordinator.

Communities in Schools' site coordinators provide integrated student support services to students who have been deemed as at risk of failing or dropping out of school. Support services offered by site coordinators range between purchasing uniforms for students in need to providing mentoring and tutoring to help students who need extra behavior support and academic support and providing parents with utility bills assistance and rental assistance to help them to maintain a stable living environment for themselves and their students. Funding from this grant could also be used to partner with nonprofit community-based organizations that provide high-quality, evidence-based wraparound services for children and implementing appropriate programs and services to address the needs of the schools.

I believe that the best way to bring about change and actual improvement in our public school education system is to implement the Communities in Schools model in all our school districts around the country. Communities In Schools' site coordinators can do way more inside of the schools than the school counselors and social workers. Site coordinators do the job of both the counselor and the school social worker and can do it in a more effective manner because they have the flexibility to work with students more frequently. The Communities in Schools' model allows for the site coordinator to be in the school every day and to be present to build relationships, strong relationships, with at-risk students. The building of these strong relationships is the most important factor in helping the students achieve greater academic success. It is the relationship that changes the child, not the programs and resources that are provided. Having Communities in Schools in school districts not only allows for the districts to have greater resources to help students but also brings more resources to parents, especially low-income single parents. Communities In Schools' site coordinators not only work with students inside the school but also provide resources for parents such as rental assistance, utility bill assistance, and brokering community resources such as tutoring, mentoring, mental health counseling among many others that help not only the student but also the entire family to function better. Communities In Schools literally surrounds students with a community of support, empowering them to succeed in school and in life.

There are so many barriers that our Black students are facing that often seem overwhelming, so much that many of us feel as though we do not have the answers to solve the issues at hand. Our students are being miseducated as you read this, being passed along without meeting the standards, and ultimately being set up for failure as they graduate from high school with diplomas that were given to them rather than having been earned. It is a shame that many of our Black students are reading well below grade level and do not have a mastery of secondary academics when they graduate from high school.

Our people have been through so much in this nation and have overcome so many barriers and obstacles just to have the opportunity to partake in the American dream, but now we are regressing, and our students are attending largely segregated schools and are receiving a poor education, one that is comparable to what was received under the worst conditions during the Jim Crow era. We do have the resources to illuminate and overcome these barriers, but we will have to do what is necessary to implement the solutions. We do this by implementing the Communities in Schools' model in all fifty states, in all school districts within those states. We have what we need to help our students succeed in school and in life. It is now time that we take advantage of it and support this national organization by asking local and state school boards to bring local affiliates into each school district in every state in the nation.

Working with Communities in Schools and allowing their model to have the far-reaching impact that it has the proven ability to do will address all the socioeconomic issues that we, as African Americans, are facing in this nation. This organization brings time-tested, evidence-based, integrated student support services that have been proven to increase academic achievement, classroom behavior, and school attendance. Increasing these three areas has also increased the promotion rate and the graduation rate in every district and state in which Communities in Schools plays a part.

Rebuilding our communities begins with education. Greater educational achievement is the only way to create a better community for future generations. The best way to prevent gentrification for those who are opposed to it is by educating our children to the best extent possible so that they may be able to rebuild their own neighborhoods through entrepreneurship and maintain them by practicing conservative values. The best way to combat police brutality in our neighborhoods is for us to create educated, law-abiding citizens who have respect for themselves and others. This will prevent the need for overly aggressive police officers to patrol our communities and interact with us in negative and, all too often, violent ways.

REFERENCES

Anyon, J. 1997. *Ghetto Schooling: A Political Economy of Urban Educational Reform*. Teachers College Press, Columbia University.

Aronson, J. and M. McGlone. 2009. "Stereotype and Social Identity Threat." In *Handbook of Prejudice, Stereotyping, and Discrimination*: 153–178. Psychology Press.

Banks, T. 2014. "Teacher Education Reform in Urban Educator Preparation Programs." *Journal of Education and Learning*. Retrieved on October 27, 2022.
https://files.eric.ed.gov/fulltext/EJ1075163.pdf

Bennett, H. 1954. "Bibb School Men Expect to Work Out Problems." *The Macon Telegraph* 01A. Microfilm Collection: Middle Georgia Regional Library Archives.

Bennett, H. 1954. "Mid-Georgia Educators Shocked at Decision". *The Macon Telegraph* 03A. Microfilm Collection: Middle Georgia Regional Library Archives.

Blanchard, Becky. 1999. "The Social Significance of Rap and Hip-Hop Culture." *Poverty and Prejudice: Media and Race*. Accessed on September 30, 2017.
https://web.stanford.edu/class/e297c/poverty_prejudice/mediarace/socialsignificance.htm.

Blankenship, D. and A. Ragusea. 2017. "Racial Concentration on the Rise in Bibb Schools." *The Macon Newsroom*.
http://macon.com/news/local/article126517089.html.

Chang, Jeff. 2005. *Can't Stop Won't Stop: A History of the Hip-Hop Generation.* New York, New York: Picador.

Centers for Disease Control and Prevention. 2022. "Supplementary Table 1: Changes in Firearm Homicide Incidence by Age Group, Race/Ethnicity, and Sex—United States, 2019–2020." https://stacks.cdc.gov/view/cdc/116520

Chuck, D., J. Yusuf, and S. Lee. 1997. *Fight the Power: Rap, Race, and Reality.* New York, New York: Delacorte Press.

Davey, D. 1999. "Why Is Rap So Powerful?" Davey D's Hip-Hop Corner.
http://www.daveyd.com/whyrapispowerart.html.

Darling-Hammond, L. 2005. "New Standards and Old Inequalities: School Reform and the Education of African American Students." In the Black Education: A Transformative Research and Action Agenda for the New Century, edited by Joyce E. King, 197–223. Mahwah, New Jersey: Lawrence Erlbaum.

Dyson, Michael Eric. 2007. *Know What I Mean?: Reflections on Hip-Hop.* New York, New York: Basic Civitas Books.

Elkouby, Sebastien. 2015. "Commercial Rap: A Pipeline to Prison?" Rap Rehab. Last modified on September 19, 2015. Accessed on September 30, 2017.
raprehab.com/commercial-rap-a-pipeline-to-prison/

———. 2016. "The Power of Hip-Hop Culture." Rap Rehab. Last modified on September 3, 2016. Accessed on September 30, 2017.
raprehab.com/rap-music-brainwashed-youth-and-the-power-of-hip-hop-culture/

Georgia Department of Education. 2008. "Bibb County School District Enrollment Report."
https://app3.doe.k12.ga.us/ows-bin/owa/fte_pack_ethnicsex.entry_form

Goodlad, J. 1991. "Why We Need a Complete Redesign of Teacher Education." *Educational Leadership*, 49(3): 4–10.

Hicks, Jeffrey. "How Hip-Hop Destroys the Potential of Black Youth." National Center for Public Policy Research. Accessed on September 30, 2017.

https://www.nationalcenter.org/P21NVHicksHipHop90706.
html

Hubbard, J. 2007. "Judge: Bibb Schools Integrated." *The Macon Telegraph* 01A. Microfilm Collection: Middle Georgia Regional Library Archives.

Lareau, A. 2003. *Unequal Childhoods: Class, Race, and Family Life.* University of California Press.

McWhorter, John H. "How Hip-Hop Holds Blacks Back." *City Journal.* Accessed on December 4, 2017. https://www.city-journal.org/html/how-hip-hop-holds-blacks-back

Meier, K. and R. England. 1984. "Black Representation and Educational Policy: Are They Related?" *American Political Science Review*, 78(2): 392–403. https://doi.org/10.2307/1963371

National Center for Science and Engineering Statistics (NCSES). 2021. "National Survey of College Graduates: 2019." NSF 22-310. Alexandria, Virginia: National Science Foundation. Available at https://ncses.nsf.gov/pubs/nsf22310/.

Ogbu, J. 1992. "Understanding Cultural Diversity and Learning." *JSTOR*, vol. 21, issue 8. https://doi.org/10.3102/0013189X021008005

Riley, J. 2014. *Please Stop Helping Us: How Liberals Make It Harder for Blacks to Succeed.* Encounter Books.

Robinson, E. 2010. *Disintegration: The Splintering of Black America.* First edition. Doubleday.

Royse, D., B. Thyer, and D. Padgett. 2018. *Program Evaluation: An Introduction to an Evidence-Based Approach.* Sixth edition. Cengage Learning.

Shakur, Tupac. 2002. "They Don't Give a Fuck About Us." AZLyrics. http://www.azlyrics.com/lyrics/tupac/theydontgiveafuckaboutus.html

Steele, C. 2010. *Whistling Vivaldi: How Stereotypes Affect Us and What We Can Do (Issues of Our Time).* W. W. Norton & Co.

Tatum, B. 2007. *Can We Talk About Race?: And Other Conversations in an Era of School Resegregation (Race, Education, and Democracy).* Boston, Massachusetts: Beacon Press.

Zuckerman, M., S. Kieffer, and C. Knee. 1998. "Consequences of Self-Handicapping: Effects on Coping, Academic Performance, and Adjustment." *Journal of Personality and Social Psychology,* 74(6): 1619–1628.
https://doi.org/10.1037/0022-3514.74.6.1619

ABOUT THE AUTHOR

Markeith Sams, MSW provides selfless service to the African American community and is passionate about addressing social issues that affect people of African ancestry. He believes selfless service means serving others without the expectation of reward. He served this nation as a soldier in the United States Army for eight years, including two tours of duty in Iraq and in his hometown of Macon, Georgia, as a firefighter and an emergency medical technician; as a Child Protective Services investigator with the Henry County Division of Family and Children Service for vulnerable youths; and as a Communities In Schools of Atlanta site coordinator and program manager. His time spent as a firefighter influenced his decision to obtain a bachelor's degree in social work from Fort Valley State University. He wanted to do more to address the ills of society that lead to the destructive trauma response afflicting many of our people. As a site coordinator for Communities in Schools, he provided integrated support services to at-risk youth, empowering them to stay in school and achieve in life. Serving others has given him a great sense of joy, and he strives to make a difference in the lives of African American youth. He received his master's degree in social work from Delaware State University. He is a school social worker in the Metro Atlanta area. This is his first book. He plans to continue advocating for policies and programs that enhance the quality of life for people of African ancestry in America and globally.

Printed in the USA
CPSIA information can be obtained
at www.ICGtesting.com
LVHW050823100823
754633LV00004B/357